OAKLAND RHAPSODY

OAKLAND R·H·A·P·S·O·D·Y

THE SECRET SOUL OF AN AMERICAN DOWNTOWN

Photographs by RICHARD NAGLER

Introduction and Commentary
by ISHMAEL REED

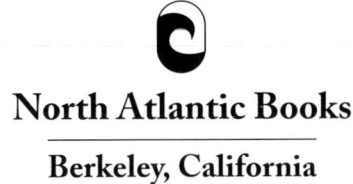

North Atlantic Books

Berkeley, California

For Sheila and Ethan and Julia

Special thanks to Peter Beren, David Charlsen, Sandy Koshkin & Barbara Levin

Oakland Rhapsody

Published by
North Atlantic Books
P.O. Box 12327
Berkeley, California 94712

Oakland Rhapsody is available in a deluxe, slipcased limited edition of one hundred copies signed and numbered by the photographer. Each limited edition book contains a signed and numbered 8" × 10" Cibachrome print entitled "Oakland and the World," which is shown on page 95. The price is $300.00 plus applicable sales tax and shipping charges. To order please contact North Atlantic Books.

Design/Production by David Charlsen
Typesetting by Jeffrey Brandenburg, ImageComp

Library of Congress Cataloging-in-Publication Data

Nagler, Richard.
    Oakland rhapsody : the secret soul of an American downtown /
photographs by Richard Nagler : introduction and text by Ishmael Reed.
        p.   cm.
    ISBN: 1-55643-197-X (cloth) : ISBN: 1-55643-196-1 (paper)
    1. Oakland (Calif.)—Pictorial works.   2. Oakland (Calif.)—
Description and travel.   I. Reed, Ishmael, 1938–   .   II. Title.
F869.02N34   1995
979.4'65—dc20   94-41629
                                                          CIP

First printing
Manufactured in Hong Kong

1 2 3 4 5 6 / 99 98 97 96 95

INTRODUCTION

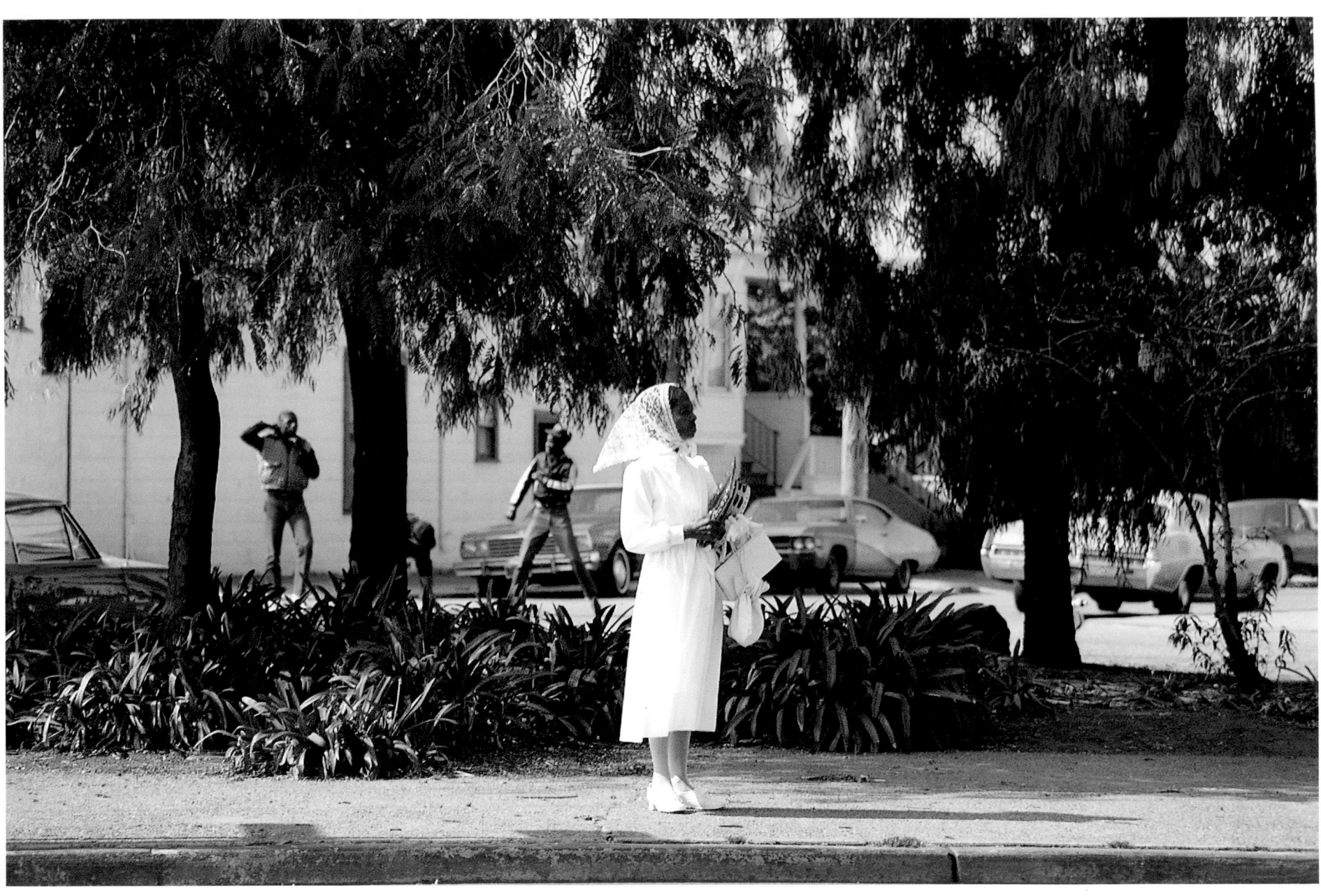

Woman in white   San Pablo Avenue near 32nd Street   *October 1982*

THE CITY THAT REFUSES TO DIE

by

Ishmael Reed

Oakland is at the crossroads. Its future is unclear. Will it be that of the black woman in white raiment, prayer book in hand, standing at the bus stop like an angelic sentinel . . . a church-going woman in white scarf, starched and stiff in white dress and white shoes, clutching her bible while behind her, three black kids are joshing around in chaotic play?

Or will it sell its soul to the false promise of progress, leaving its humanity behind like Nagler's forgotten men, sleeping on benches, living in doorways? One expects that a city that has survived catastrophes both man-made and natural will survive. Oakland refuses to die.

Downtown Oakland serves as a metaphor for the entire city — its wealth and its poverty, its decay and its renewal, its hasty development and its neglected tradition.

By concentrating on its downtown, Richard Nagler has captured the beauty, the despair, and the contradictions of Oakland. One of the ways he explores these contradictions is by using contrast. In one photo a black man lies on a bench. On a wall behind him are llamas painted in the style of the animals in the caves of Lascaux. Looming over him, its architectural lines resembling Darth Vader's, is the Clorox Building. Abstract, impersonal. This photo speaks volumes about how the human spirit and nature have been overwhelmed by development.

Like the poet, Nagler has an eye for paradox. Nagler is also an archivist. The Victorian houses and their accessories, which invoke a grander period in Oakland's history, are shown in a state of deterioration. Nagler reveres the past . . . the ornate doorways . . . the entrance to the mosque-like Fox Theatre whose Saturday matinees were attended by Japanese American author Toshio Mori. Nagler notices the details that have been lost in the stressful frenzy that is modern life . . . the precious curios in forgotten windows. A black woman resting her head against a wall in seeming frustration is engulfed by lines . . . the yellow line of the street, the lines of the sidewalk, the lines which border the fence topped with barbed wire. It is a short story whose message is that the lives of some black Oaklanders are frustrated by the limitations they must face. The cold, unfeeling downtown buildings dwarf these people as nature does the people in the paintings of the Hudson River school. But the Clorox Building is not a mountain.

In this Oakland of transition the old and new seem to collide. To the former occupants of the ghettos they peddled root beer; now it's a new and vicious form of alcohol.

A man, donned in what appears to be a scuba diver's headgear, refurbishes some Victorian columns as lions with rings in their mouths look on, horrified. But most of the time the people and their surroundings seem to be in sync. A youngster playfully jabs at an adult in front of old signs representing the names of famous boxing champions. Perhaps this lad's name will be there one day.

The street becomes ancient Greek theatre. If Nagler isn't aware of these incongruities, then he is certainly lucky.

You wonder how Nagler matches these phenomena, how he matches the colors of the pedestrians with that of their surroundings. The tomato red of a woman's helmet-styled umbrella with the reds of the wall behind her. The man's green cap which compliments the green of the art on the wall next to him. The wall's eyes seem to be watching him. As in the cases of the Victorians, inanimate objects are the witnesses to history. Or are they alive?

Is that a movie theatre being razed, or a ship whose head is decorated by a woman wielding a sword? An older woman walks by. She's just had her hair done. Is she wearing bell bottoms? The kind they wear in the navy?

But like Oakland, a city that refuses to die, some can not be overwhelmed by false progress or catastrophe. An Asian man in grey shirt and black pants sits at the bottom of a brick wall that towers over him. A sign at the top asks, "Why?" A little girl peeks out of a window on which Santa Claus pictures are pasted. There is no snow, only concrete covering the lawn. I sometimes miss the snow. The eastern winter which, unlike Oakland's, is clearly distinguishable from other seasons. But who would trade Nagler's raspberry clouds at sunset for a snowstorm in Vermont?

At first, I wasn't very happy about moving into Oakland. Though I have received compliments for not abandoning the black community, I actually came into Oakland as a regentrifier. California home prices being what they are, the huge pigeon-infested, dilapidated Victorian that I bought and renovated was a steal. But after a while, I discovered that even with its problems, problems that the media always seem eager to document, for me, someone who travels throughout the United States, extensively, of all the cities in America, I find Oakland to be the most desirable.

I left the east, where I grew up, in 1967. After I taught at Harvard in 1987, I concluded that all of the reasons that I left the east, including the intense enmity between white and black ethnics, and the depressing gray skies, were valid.

I once heard a writer say that he was glad that Oakland had a bad image because he didn't want those Yuppies from Berkeley moving to Oakland in droves. When we held town meetings to oppose the relocation of an upscale theatre into Oakland, we described the outfit as a Trojan horse for a Yuppie invasion that would disrupt its multicultural diversity. Yuppies have been described as those who are "utterly devoid of ethnicity." They would be out of place here because it's multiethnicity that is perhaps Oakland's most attractive feature. Formerly those who streamed into Oakland for job opportunities were white and African American ethnics. Others, who saw Oakland as a city of refuge, came to escape the 1906 earthquake: Italian American, Portuguese, German, Irish. One of the streets which borders my neighborhood is called Genoa. Recently, Oakland has drawn immigrants from Vietnam, Korea, and China. In the San Antonio district of Oakland, thirty-four different languages are spoken. It is Oakland's multiethnicity, I believe, that gained for it the position of fifteenth among America's most desirable cities in which to live.

Oakland's critics took this news to mean that the United States is in worse shape than anybody ever thought, because of the problems that dog Oakland: unemployment, drugs, and crime. 1992's homicide rate is threatening to exceed that of 1991 when the homicide rate was one hundred sixty-five. In addition, an ambitious downtown development scheme seems to have become the victim of economic slump. One of the reasons that the late Robert Maynard, the only black publisher of a major American daily, had to sell the *Oakland Tribune* was that the much-touted downtown Renaissance hadn't materialized.

The introduction of crack cocaine in the middle 1980s has produced a high homicide rate and a climate of fear resulting from the warfare between crack dealers over their markets. The people of my North Oakland neighborhood where, like many other neighborhoods, blacks, whites, and yellows live in relative peace, are no longer astonished when they hear the bursts from semiautomatic weapons.

Of course, these drug peddlers, many of them children, are following the tradition of the white ethnics of previous generations, who felt that the legitimate routes to success were denied to them. A crack dealer on my block said that he turned to selling the drug because the baby food factory where he worked had closed. The participation of Jewish, Italian, Irish, and German Americans in the multibillion dollar underground economy helped to ease their group's way into the suburbs. This, of course, is not to excuse criminality, but the media and the government have a tendency to dismiss the drug epidemic as a black problem, when 80% of the consumers of drugs in this country are white. According to the New York United States Attorney, twenty-two ethnic groups are involved in the drug trade. American banks and industries also benefit from the drug trade through money laundering and by supplying chemicals to those who process the drugs. The accounts of four local banks were frozen when they were discovered to have belonged to the Colombian cartel.

It was my comments about the Oakland drug mess, printed in the *San Francisco Examiner/Chronicle's* "Image" magazine, that gained me an audience with some of the most powerful business and political figures in Oakland. They were concerned about my giving Oakland a bad name and discouraging investors in "the Oakland Renaissance." Only a small percentage of Oakland residents are employed by these downtown industries. I was told that Oakland has a solid economic base, and, indeed, new hotels, office buildings, shopping malls, and other retail and commercial outlets are continuing to spring up. The most spectacular development is the City Center, a $650 million, twelve-block project in the middle of the downtown. The construction of a $142 million federal building is now complete.

Preservation Park, a $13 million project which involves the restoration of sixteen Victorian homes, has also been finished. The multicultural literary organization, of which I am Chairman of the Board, is located there.

Downtown businessmen and politicians hope that these merchandising centers and other developments, including a $225 million Chinatown Redevelopment Project, will draw thousands of people into Oakland within the next few years. Whether this will happen remains a question. One development, Old Oakland, a $50 million project which involved the restoration of eleven Victorian buildings, has gone bankrupt, but new owners are beginning to fill the space.

Support among Oaklanders for the downtown Renaissance is less than unanimous; residents of the neighborhoods maintain that downtown development has diverted attention and financial aid from their needs. Brenda Payton, columnist and gadfly of the downtown establishment, speaks for many when she wonders whether investing in stadiums, office space, and conference centers, instead of in more innovative projects, was a mistake.

Other factors contributing to the down side of Oakland's image is an educational system that is in such a mess and rocked by scandals — some school employees have been indicted — that it had to be placed in state trusteeship. There is a feeling among the neighborhoods, many of them poor, that the downtown Renaissance has passed them by, and has favored white commuters who take the cash out of Oakland and into the white suburbs. Yes, many of us criticize Oakland, and I have to such an extent that the black city manager phoned me and asked me to try to think positively about Oakland.

––––––––––––––––––––––––––

Oakland is probably the best-kept secret in the United States.

In the middle of the city lies the gem of Oakland, Lake Merritt, which sparkles with seductive colors at twilight, a scene enhanced by a necklace of lights which surround the lake. Citizens raised a million dollars to restore the lights which had gone dark during World War II. Watching the lit skyline from the east side of the lake at twilight is to experience a beauty that makes one forget about Oakland's problems.

The weather brings a feast to the skin as soothing breezes circulate the city. Some of those remind me of the spicy, healing breezes from the Gulf of Mexico that tantalize Galveston, Texas. Oakland's architectural history is rich with a character that many cities would envy. Some parts of downtown residential Oakland resemble California of the 1940s which is the reason that Francis Ford Coppola gave for shooting scenes for his film, "Tucker." An old Oakland movie palace, The Grand Lake, has been restored to its former splendor. Other sections include those Victorians and Gothic gables whose decay Richard Nagler has captured so well. They remind us of the ancient Oakland of merchant princes, railroaders, sailors, and Klondikers. One of the Klondikers was Jack London — novelist, short story writer, and boxing buff.

Jack London was one of many writers who have made Oakland the literary capital of California, having hosted at one time or another an array of Gertrude Stein, Robert Louis Stevenson, Brete Harte, Jessica Mitford, Maya Angelou, Kay Boyle, Floyd Salas, Reginald Lockett, and Leslie Scalapino. One of Oakland's tourist attractions is Jack London Square, located near Brete Harte Boardwalk, where one may find one of America's supreme Louisiana gumbo and jambalaya palaces, T.J.'s The Gingerbread House.

Oakland cuisine ranges from black southern soul food to Thai, and one of the favorite hangouts is the Downtown Hofbrau on Broadway, located near the Paramount Theater. The Paramount has been magnificently restored to its original Art Deco style. Oakland also boasts an active nightlife where visitors can hear the blues or dance to salsa or the soca.

Oakland is composed of nine districts: San Antonio, North Oakland, West Oakland, Fruitvale, The Upper Hills, Elmhurst, Chinatown, Central East Oakland, and the Lower Hills — each with its own rich history. They range from the affluent Oakland Hills where the median income is $68,851 and the unemployment rate is 2.8%, to the poorest district, West Oakland, where the median income is $15,265 and the unemployment rate is 19.8%. What West Oakland lacks in money it makes up for with culture and history. The First African Methodist Episcopal Church was founded there in 1852. During the 1940s, blacks from Louisiana and Texas found jobs there as factory and ship workers. Pullman car porters settled in West Oakland and played an important role in its history. Black Panther founder Huey Newton was a West Oaklander.

Oakland refuses to die. Near the anniversary of the worst earthquake since 1906, the Upper Hills were the scene of America's worst urban fire. The October 17, 1989 earthquake, which damaged many of Oakland's downtown buildings including City Hall, built in 1912 during the administration of Mayor Mott, the Flatiron Building, and the historic Hotel Oakland where Charles Lindbergh and Herbert Hoover were once guests, brought a catastrophe from which Oakland still hasn't recovered. Writer William Lawson, whose home was destroyed in the fire, captured the despair of that moment in a *San Francisco Examiner* op-ed piece: "At the remains of our house, thousands of exquisitely beautiful white ash ghosts of our books, crumble to nothing at the touch of the wind. Deep down, the pile still glows orange, a waning of Sunday's unbelievable mad physics."

If buildings made a city, then clearly Oakland would be in trouble. Fortunately, it's the people who make the city, people whom Richard Nagler has captured with wit and compassion. With his portraits of alienated individuals, actors in a city undergoing transition, Nagler may well be the Edward Hopper of the camera.

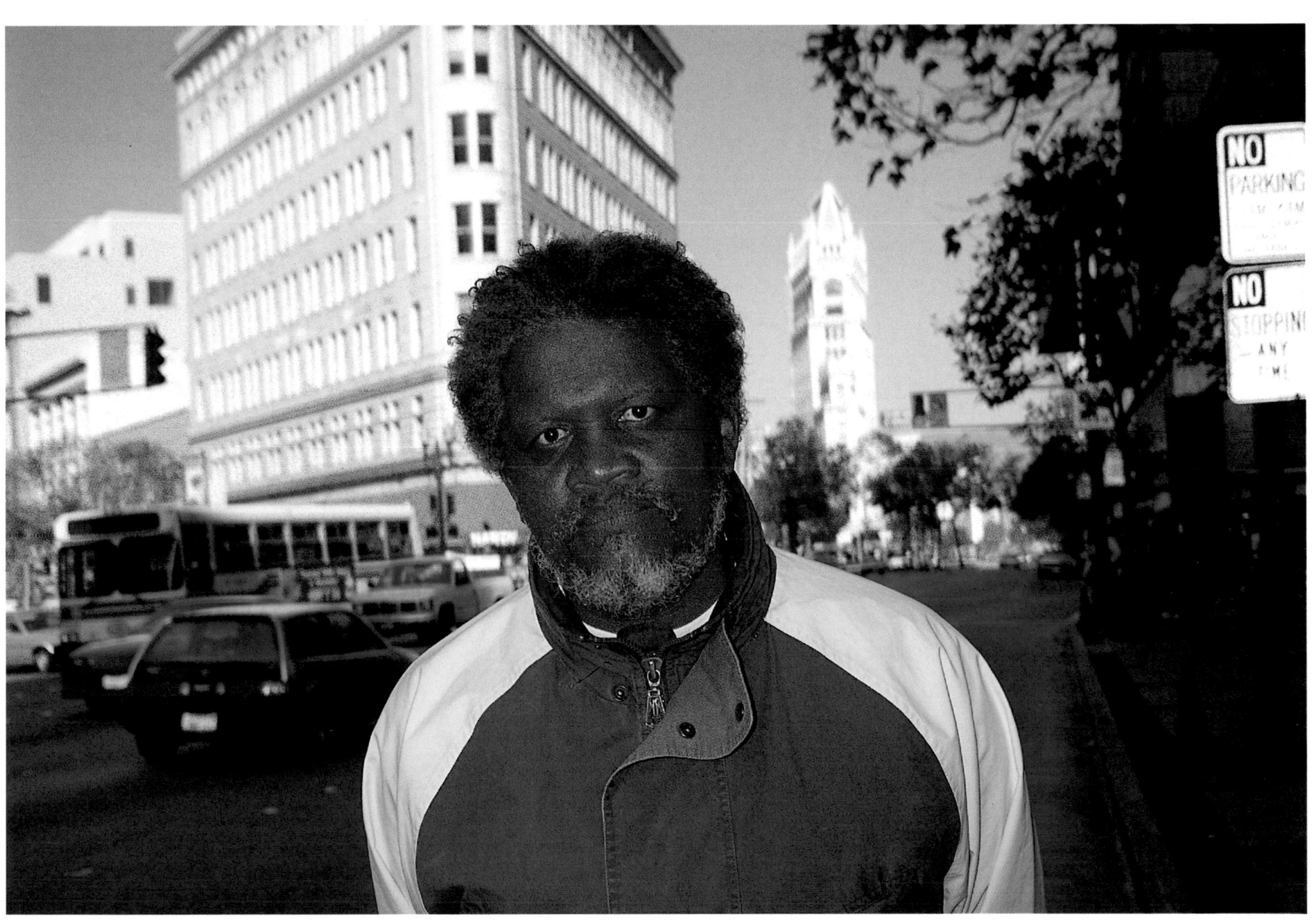

Ishmael Reed 14th and Broadway *November 1992*

PHOTOGRAPHER'S NOTES

My dictionary defines a rhapsody as "an instrumental composition of free, irregular form, suggesting improvisation." The photographs in this book are rhapsodic in the sense that they were taken with the desire to convey the vibrant melodies and rhythms of life on the street in Downtown Oakland. In the music world, Oakland is known as "Rap City," but to me, Oakland is a rhapsody: it reverberates with gospel, jazz, salsa, reggae, and Asian compositions, as well as rap.

I have organized my photographic rhapsody about Downtown Oakland into four movements:

The Transition contains photographs taken between 1975 and 1984 which show a small town growing up, its inhabitants and architecture caught between Oakland's past and its future. Along with the extraordinary quality of the light in the downtown, I was intrigued by the architecture and the signage which provide a living course in urban archaeology and the human condition.

San Pablo Avenue, which leads into downtown, evolved from an Indian trail into a broad boulevard. Over the years the street has moved from glamour to neglect, but it serves for me as a metaphor for Oakland's chaos and character. The many churches along the avenue are depositories of inspiring faith and soul, and they rock the street with gospel while, just outside, crack dealers and prostitutes work their trades.

A Few Words About Oakland is an excerpt from a larger body of photographs in which I have attempted to capture an accidental encounter between an isolated word and a person who somehow enters the picture frame. These are difficult pictures to take, sometimes they take weeks to realize, but I find the sum total of the words provide an intriguing visual poem about life in Oakland.

The Here and Now are my photographs of Downtown Oakland in the present. I have tried to include pictures which reinforce Oakland's wonderful diversity in its architecture and multiculturalism. It's a great city, star-crossed at times, but resplendent in its light and location, and, as Ishmael Reed so wisely calls it, it is "The City That Refuses To Die."

I asked Ishmael Reed, one of America's finest poets and novelists, to introduce each movement with a poem which expresses his reactions to the photography and his feelings about Downtown Oakland.

Whenever I read his words or heard Ishmael Reed speak over the years, I always felt that his emotional response to his adopted hometown felt astonishingly parallel to the photographs I was taking. In his many essays and public appearances, he has been a consistent champion of Oakland's uniqueness and a stalwart critic of Oakland's failings.

I had the pleasure of working with Isaac Bashevis Singer on a previous book, and I am honored as well to have had the brilliant collaboration of Ishmael Reed on *Oakland Rhapsody*. Reed, like Isaac Singer, is one of our most original thinkers and writers, and his generous prose in the introduction and his powerful poetry throughout the book have given *Oakland Rhapsody* an important blend of the verbal with the visual.

OAKLAND RHAPSODY

THE TRANSITION

An old man leans upon a pillar of the past.
He and the building which supports him are about to be zapped by time.
They are not the only ones.
A black man, one of those endangered species, sits in the doorway. He looks
    depressed. Unemployed, maybe.

Just as the old man, the black man, and Nagler's ever-present Victorians are about to
    be consigned to oblivion,
so are the old barber pole and the barbershop,
where the barber may have been acquainted with three generations of customers.
The Victorians are trapped in the Bail Bondsman's window.

Romare Bearden would appreciate Richard Nagler's Oakland. Look carefully in the
    face of Oakland and you will see a Mayan eye, a Benin jaw, or a Scandinavian
    forehead.

Mark Morris says that when you walk down the street and you're listening to music
    you're dancing. The young black men in Nagler's pictures, confident, energetic,
    don't need the music.

— Ishmael Reed

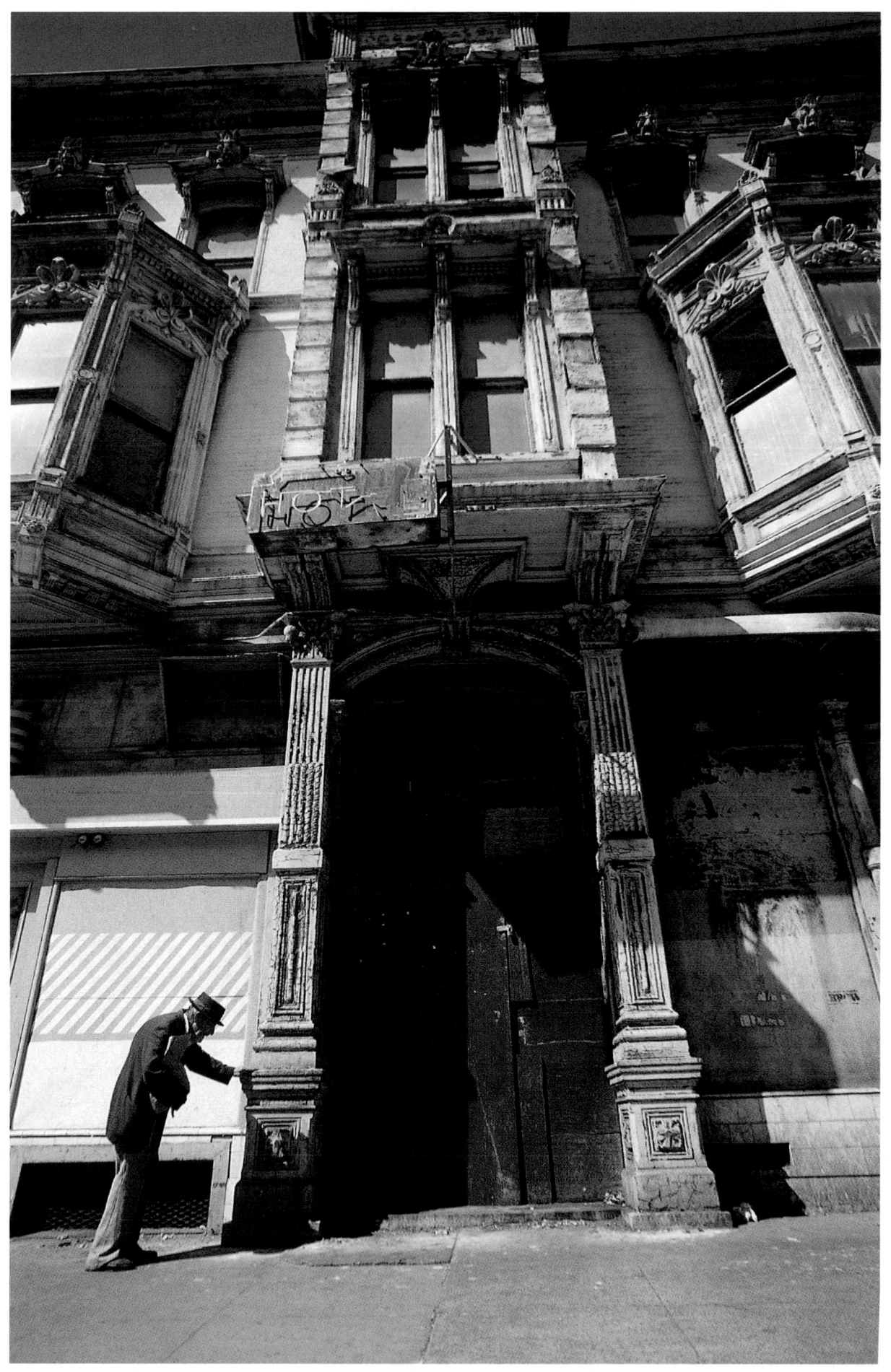

Old man, old hotel   9th and Washington   *July 1977*

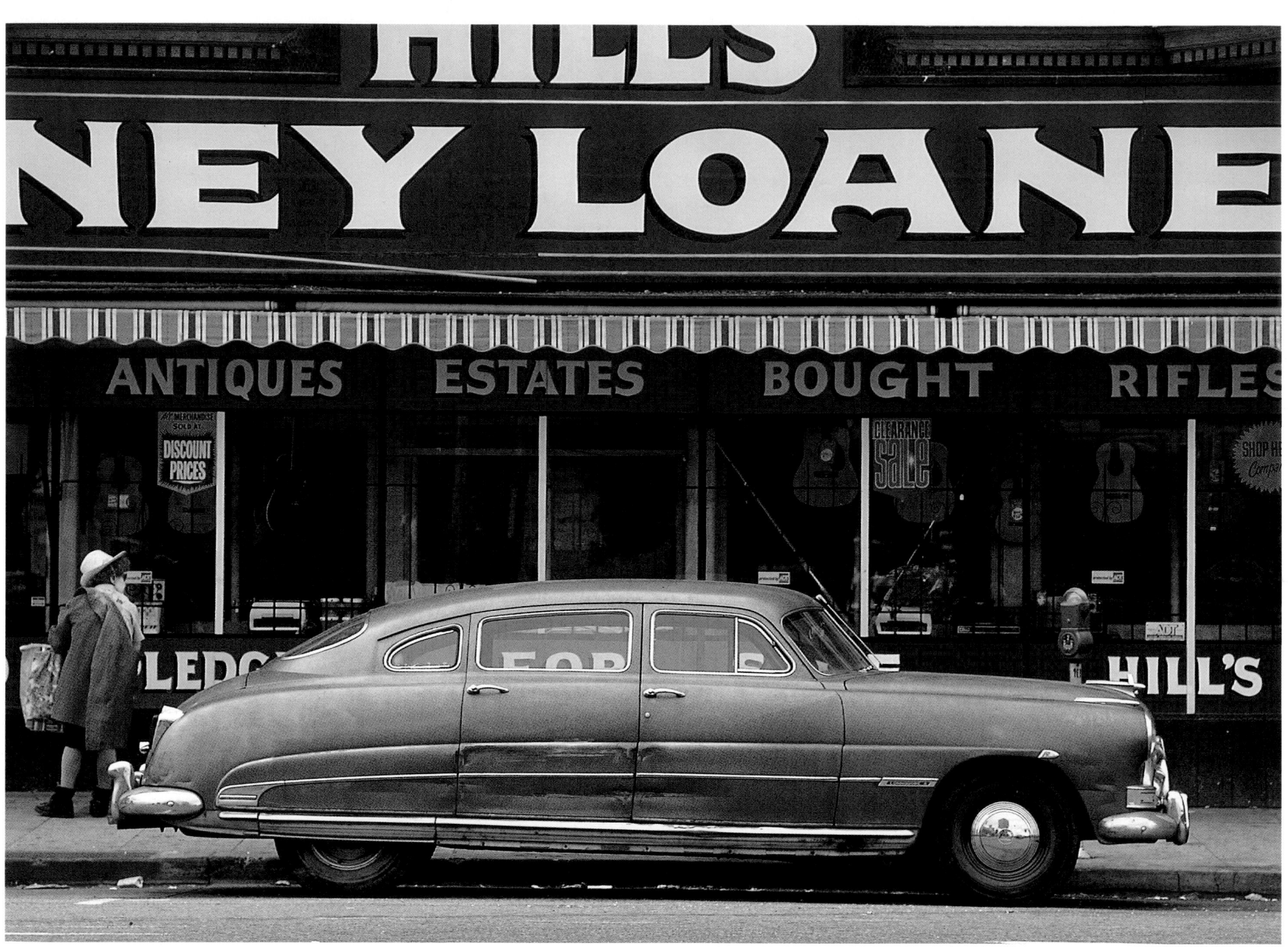

Hudson   10th and Broadway   *September 1980*

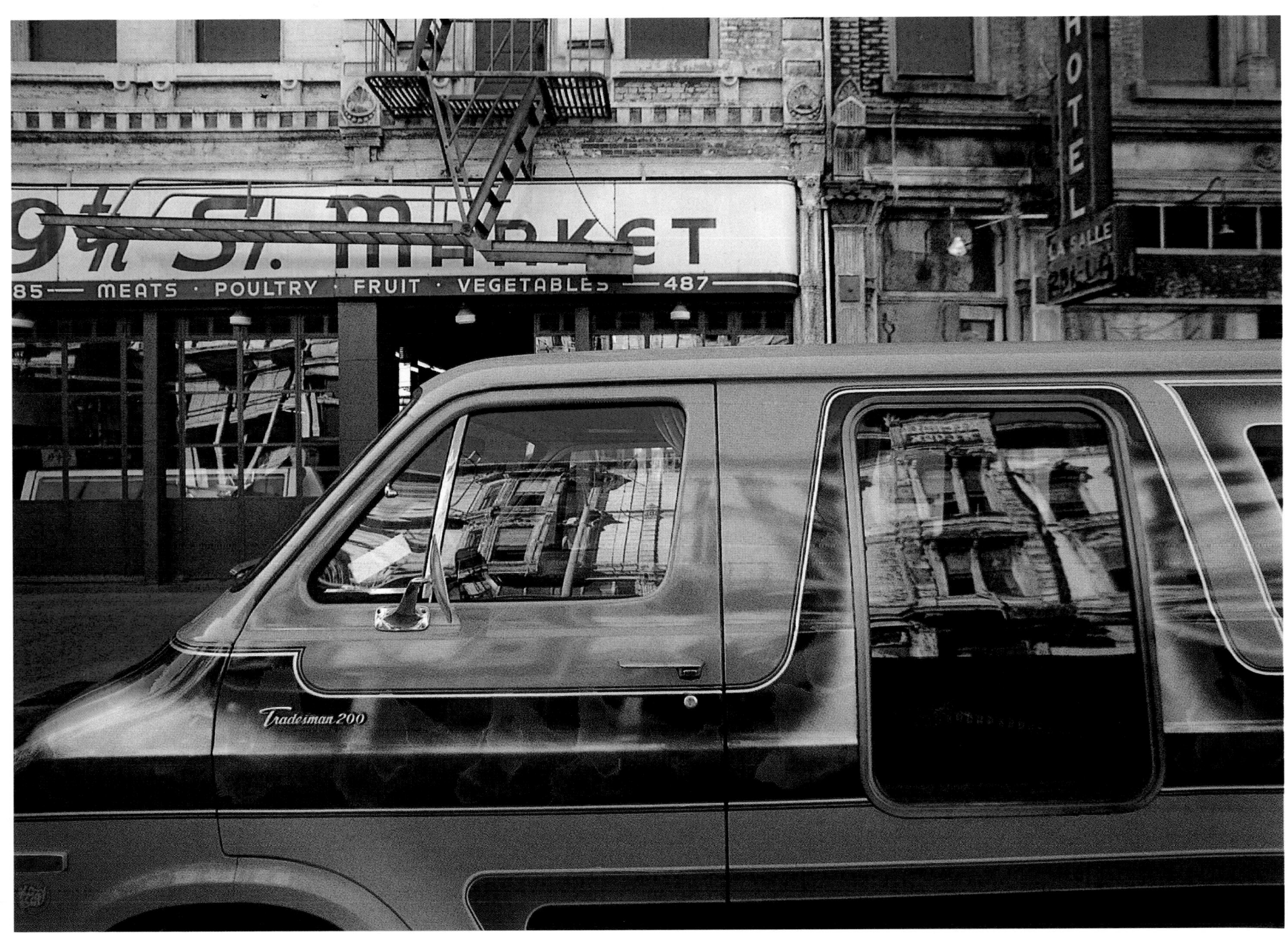

Van Reflections   9th Street   *December 1978*

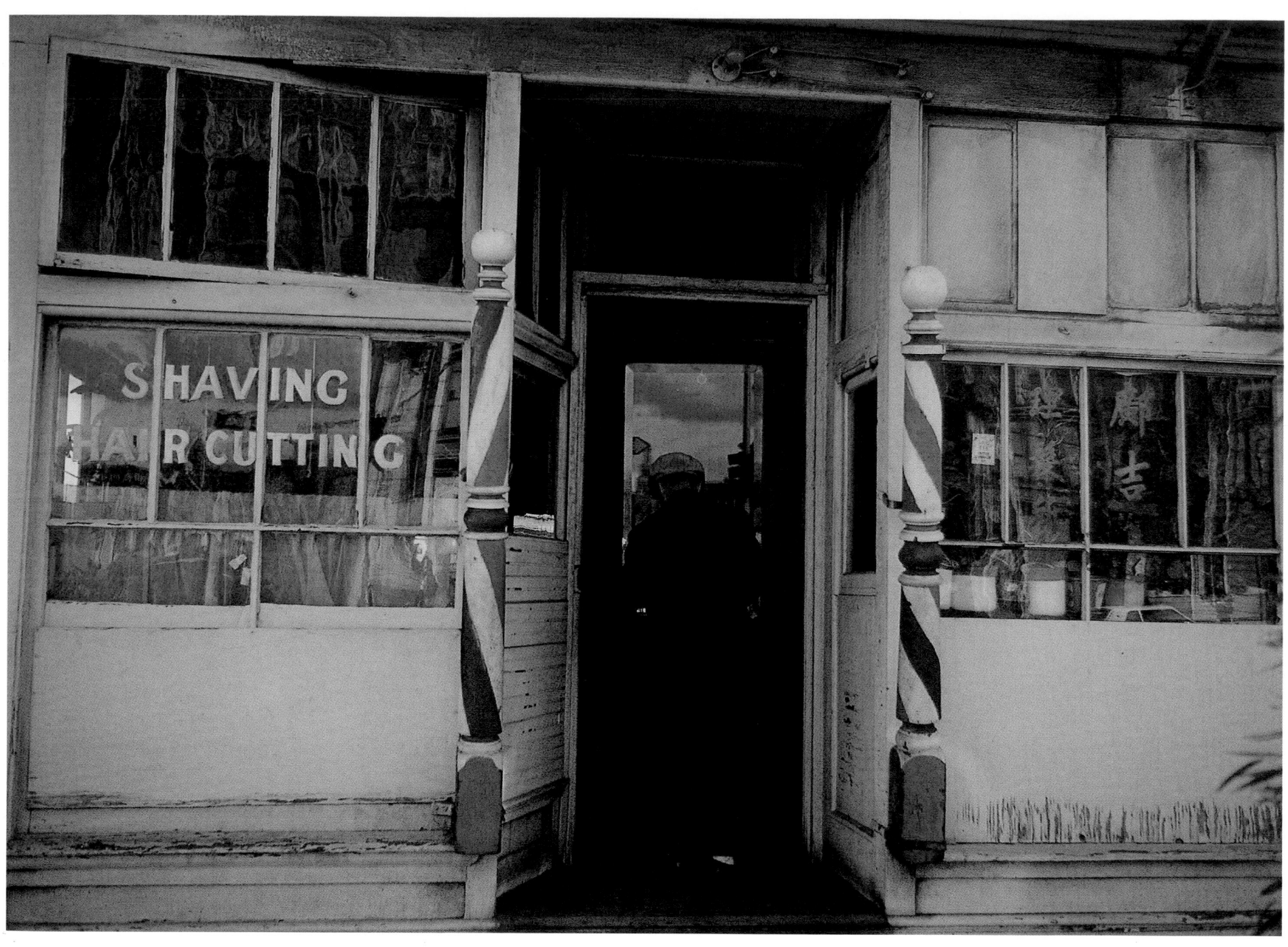

Chinatown Barbershop   8th and Harrison   *April 1975*

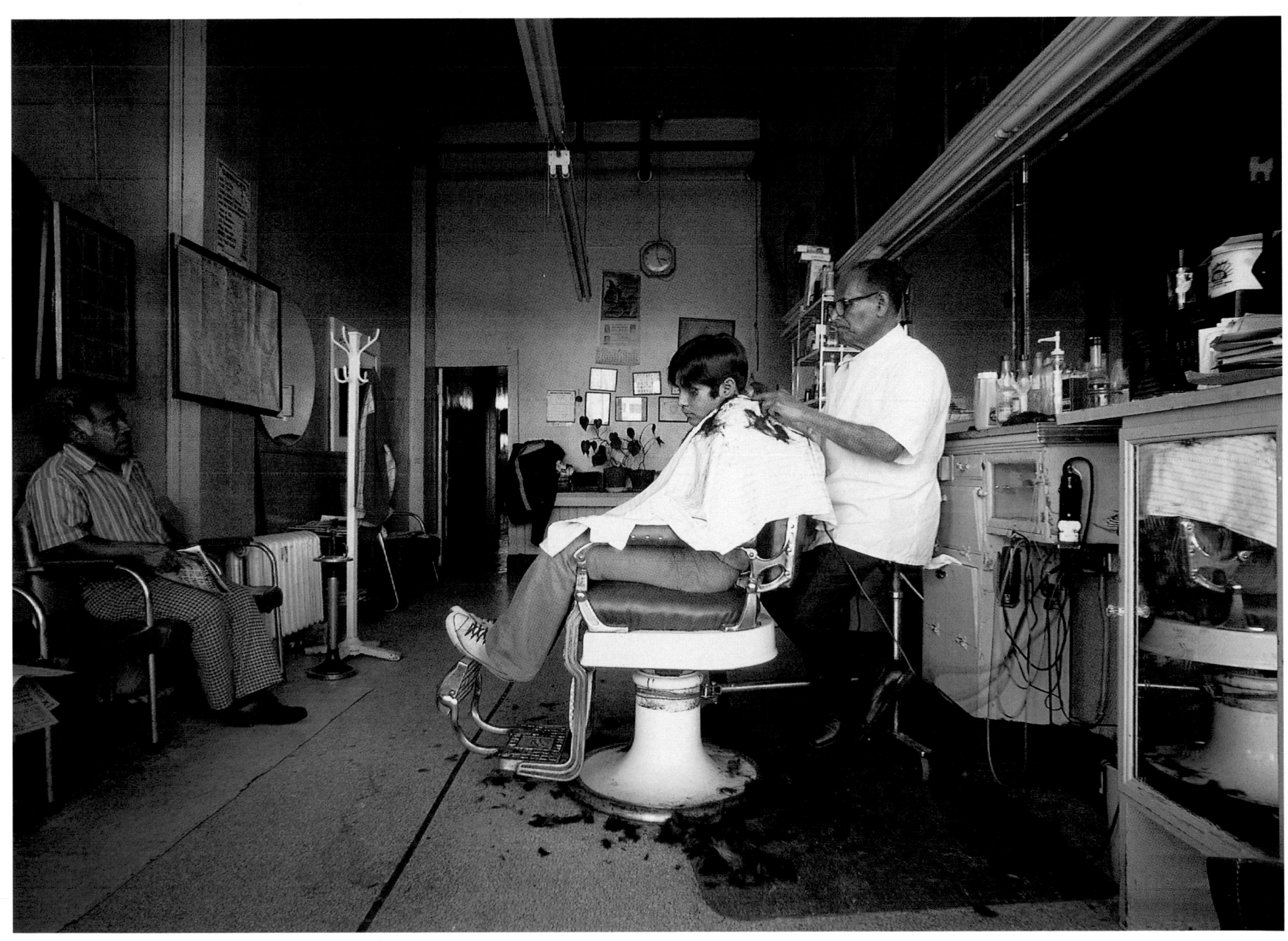

Barbershop   8th Street near Broadway   *March 1977*

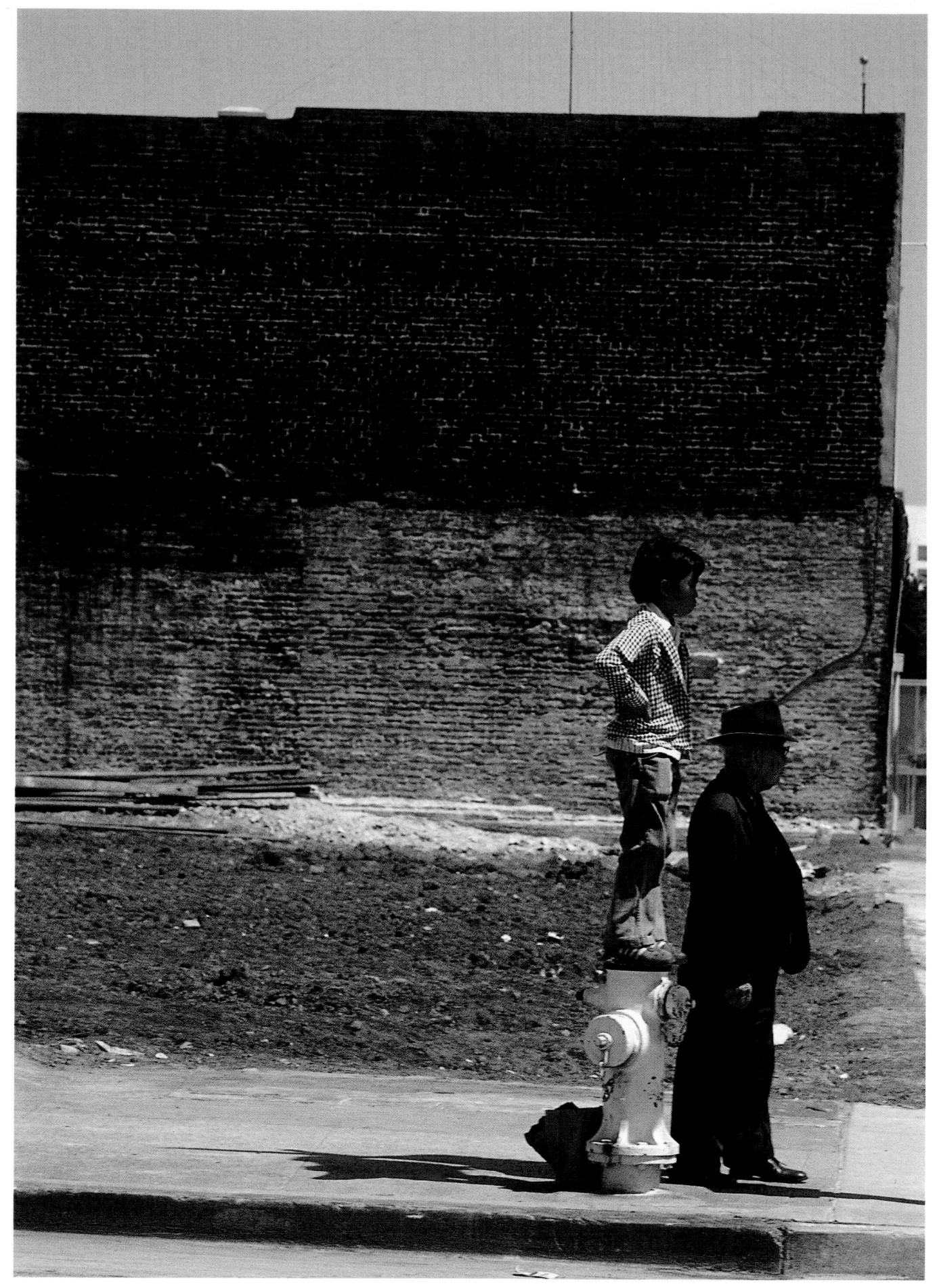

Waiting for the bus Chinatown, 9th and Franklin *August 1979*

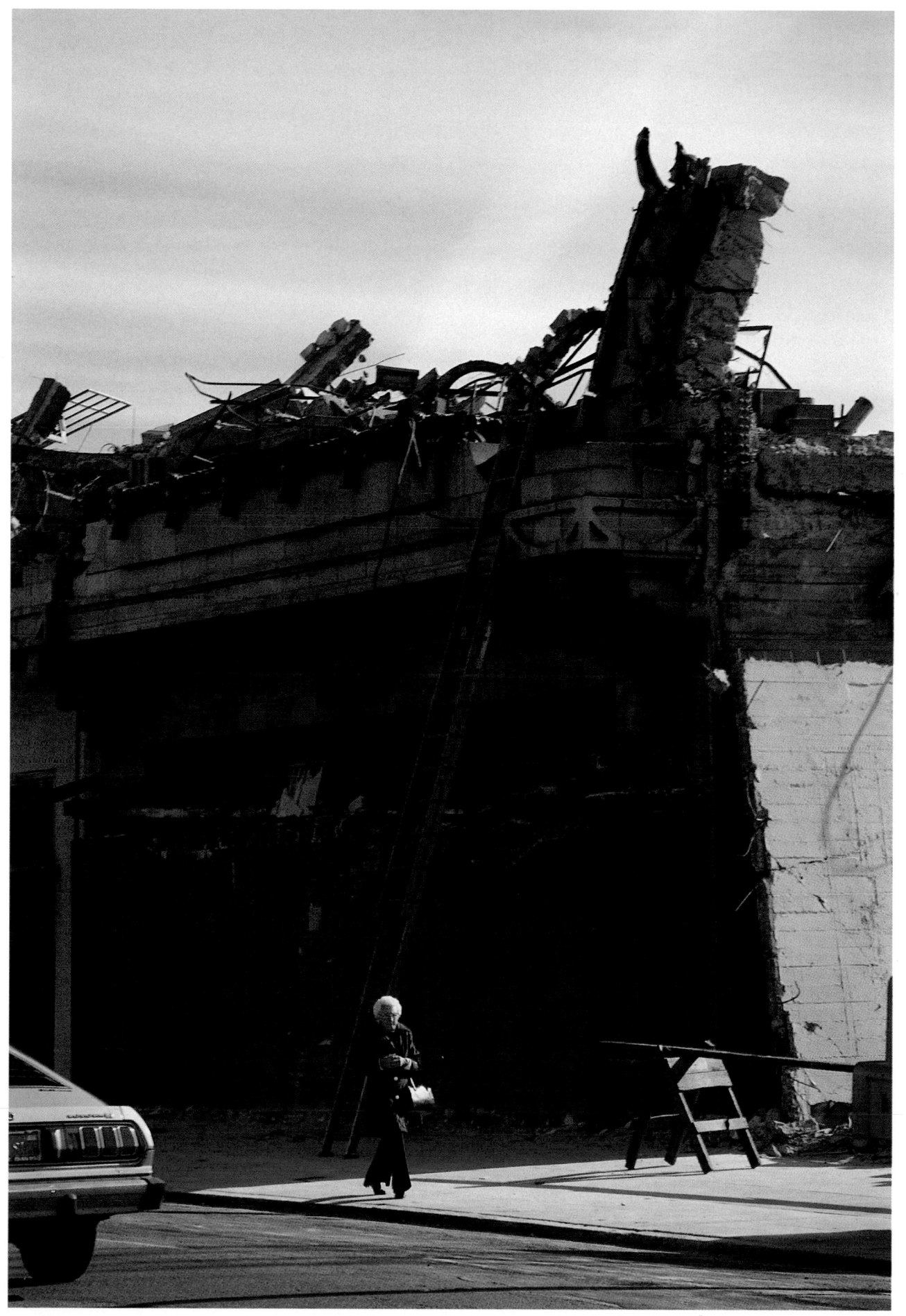

Demolition of the T & D Theatre   11th near Broadway   *January 1979*

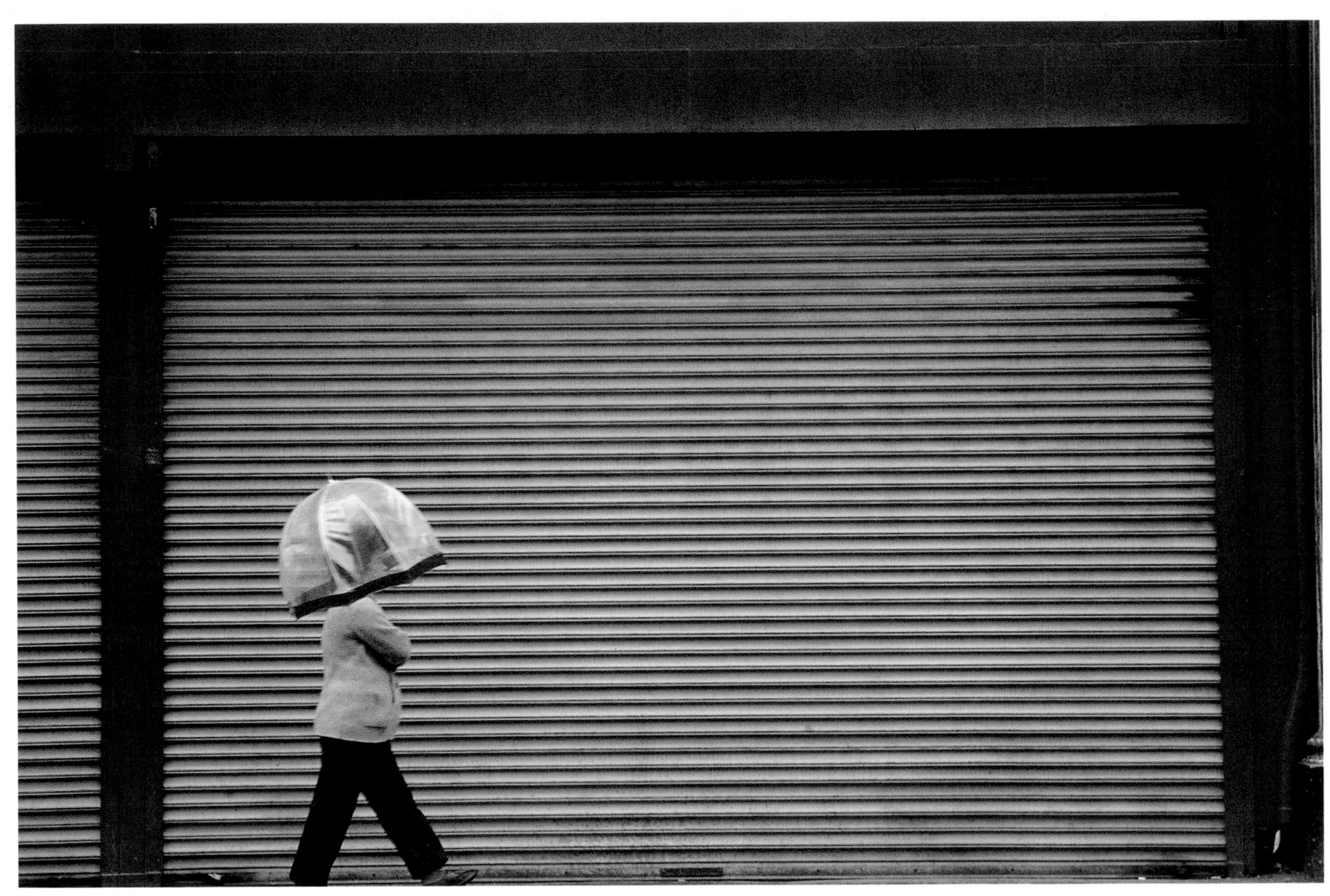

Woman framed in red   9th near Broadway   *May 1983*

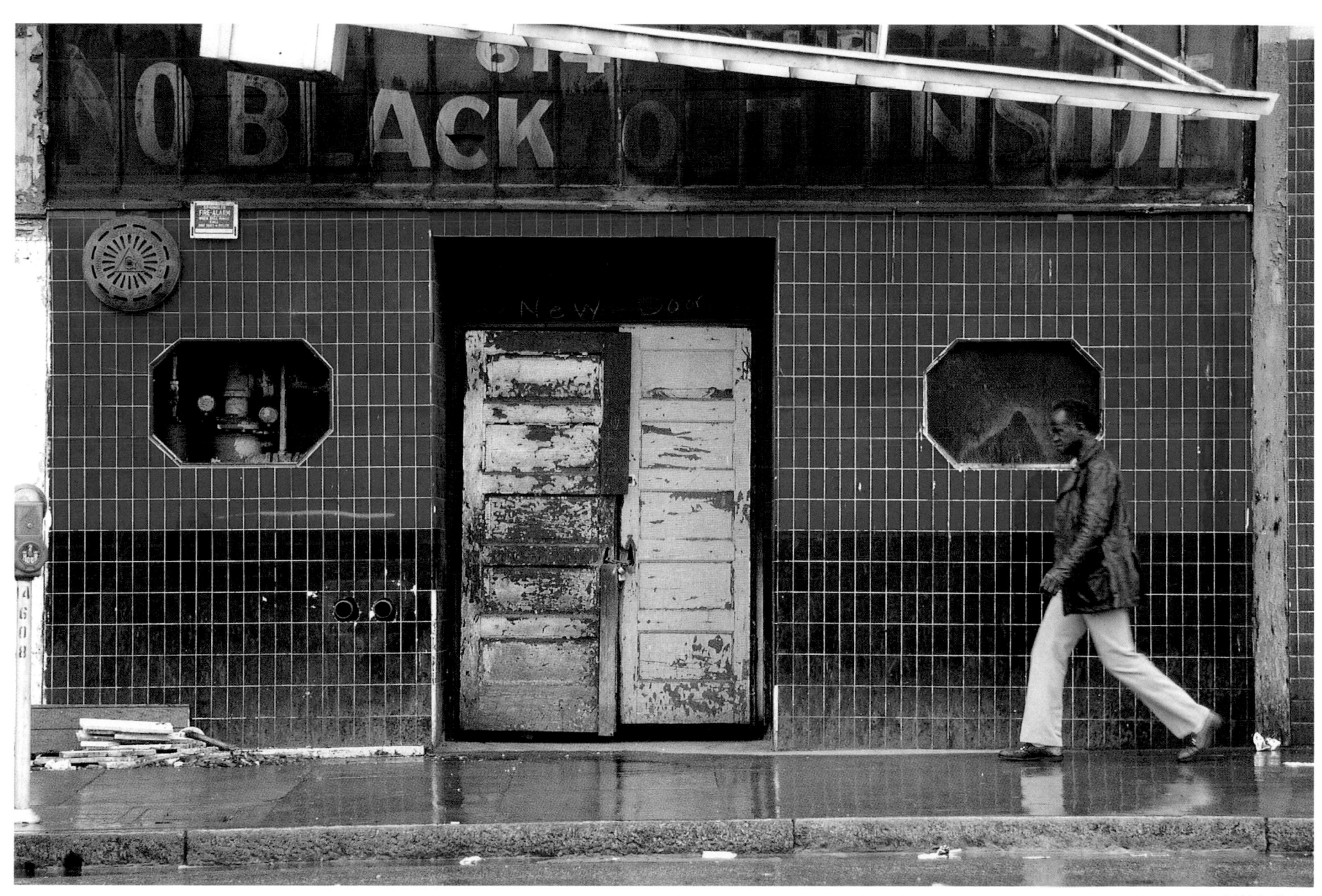

No Blackout Inside   14th Street at Jefferson   *March 1981*

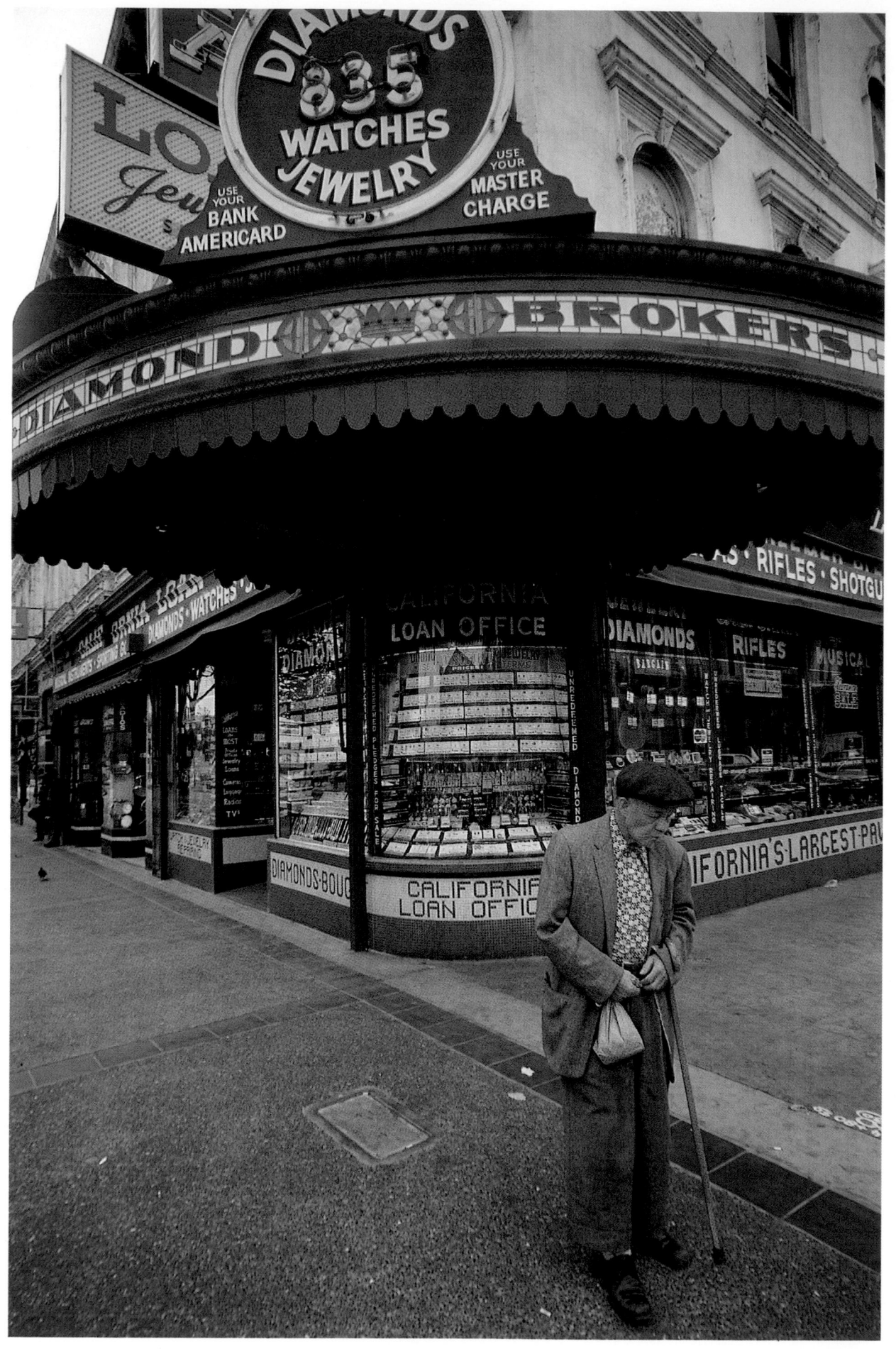

California Loan Office   9th and Broadway   *November 1980*

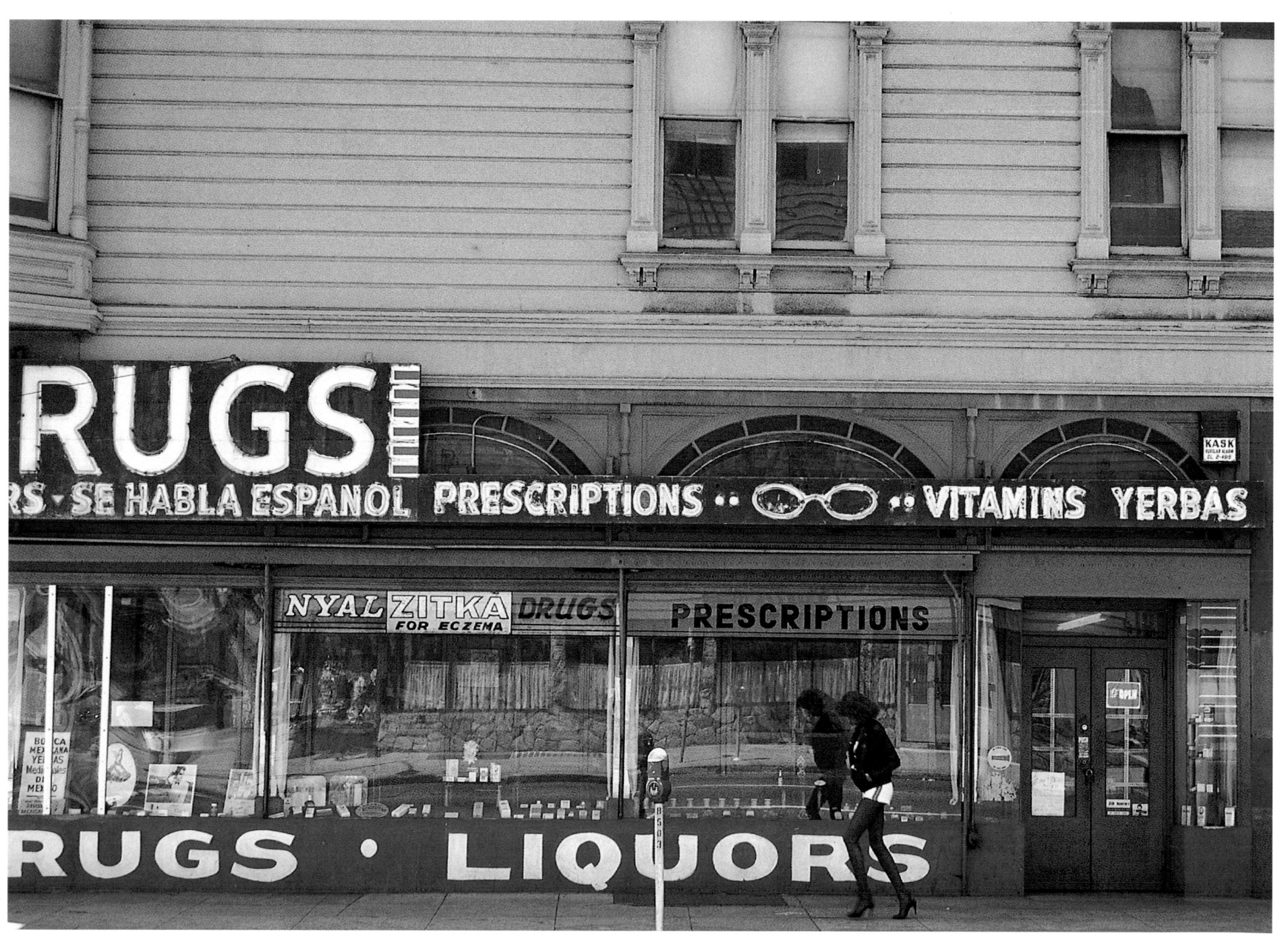

Drug Store   8th and Washington   *August 1982*

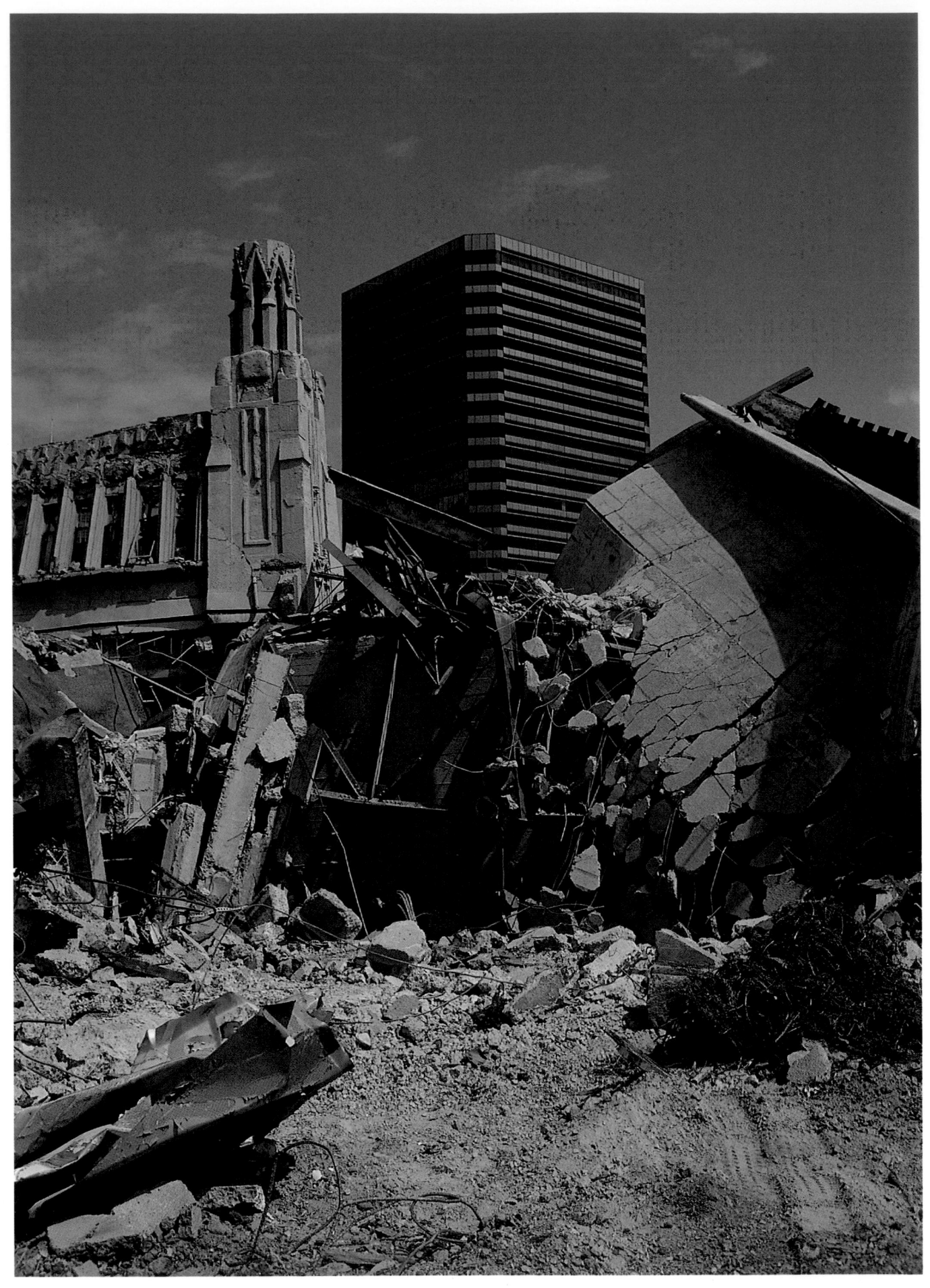

Demolition 12th and Clay *March 1977*

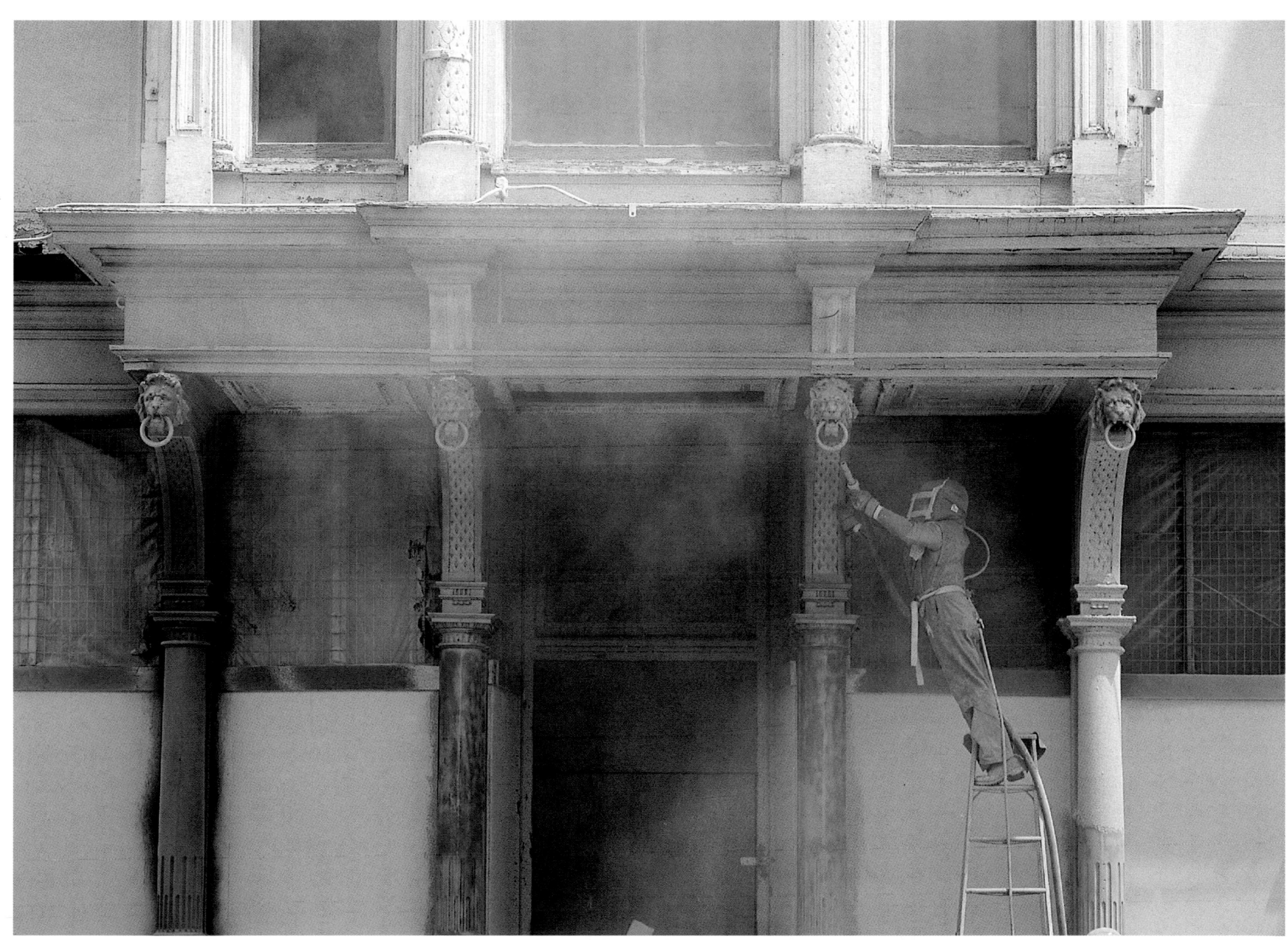

Spaceman   on Ninth Street   *May 1983*

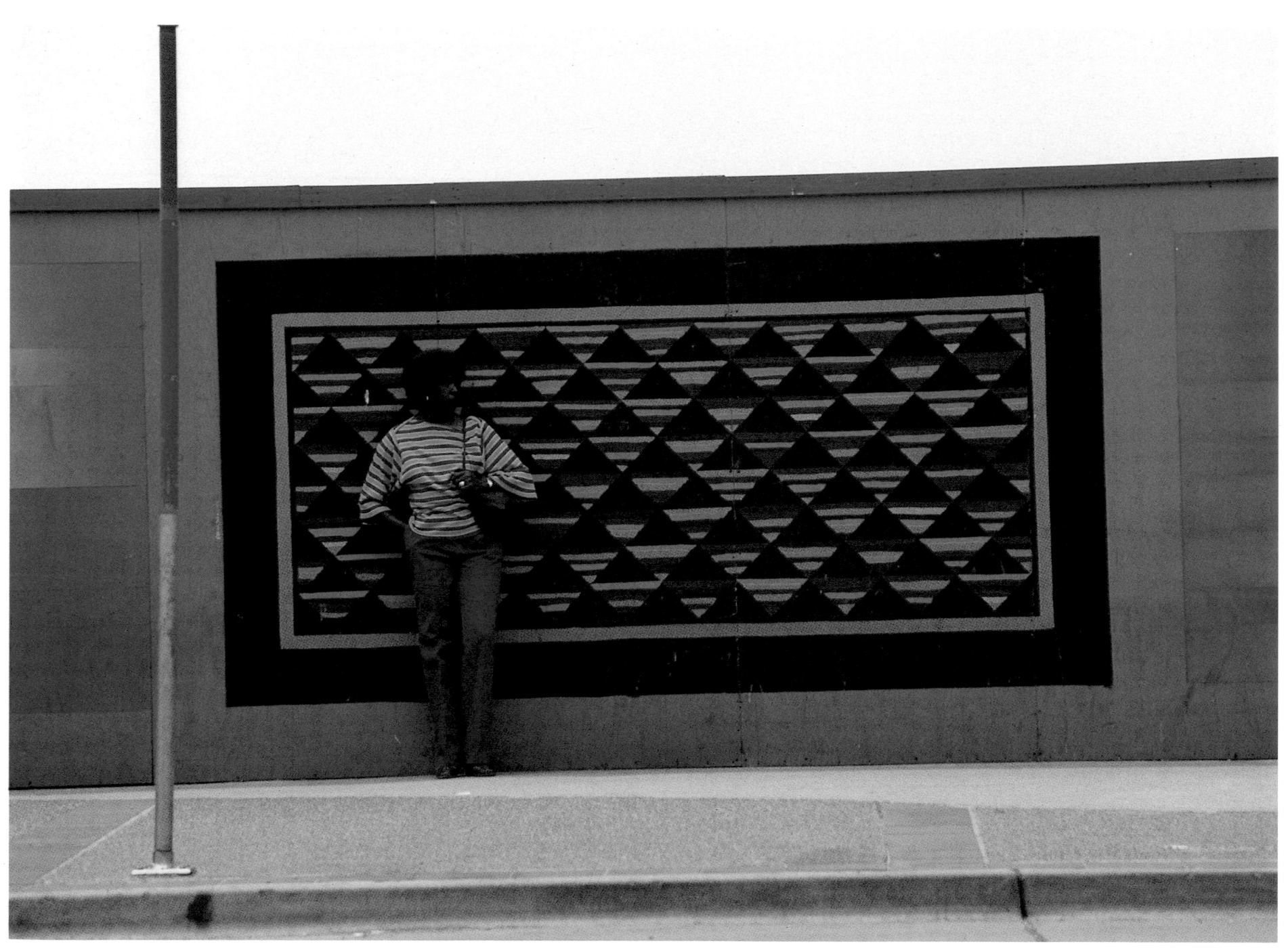

Waiting for the bus   11th and Broadway   *May 1983*

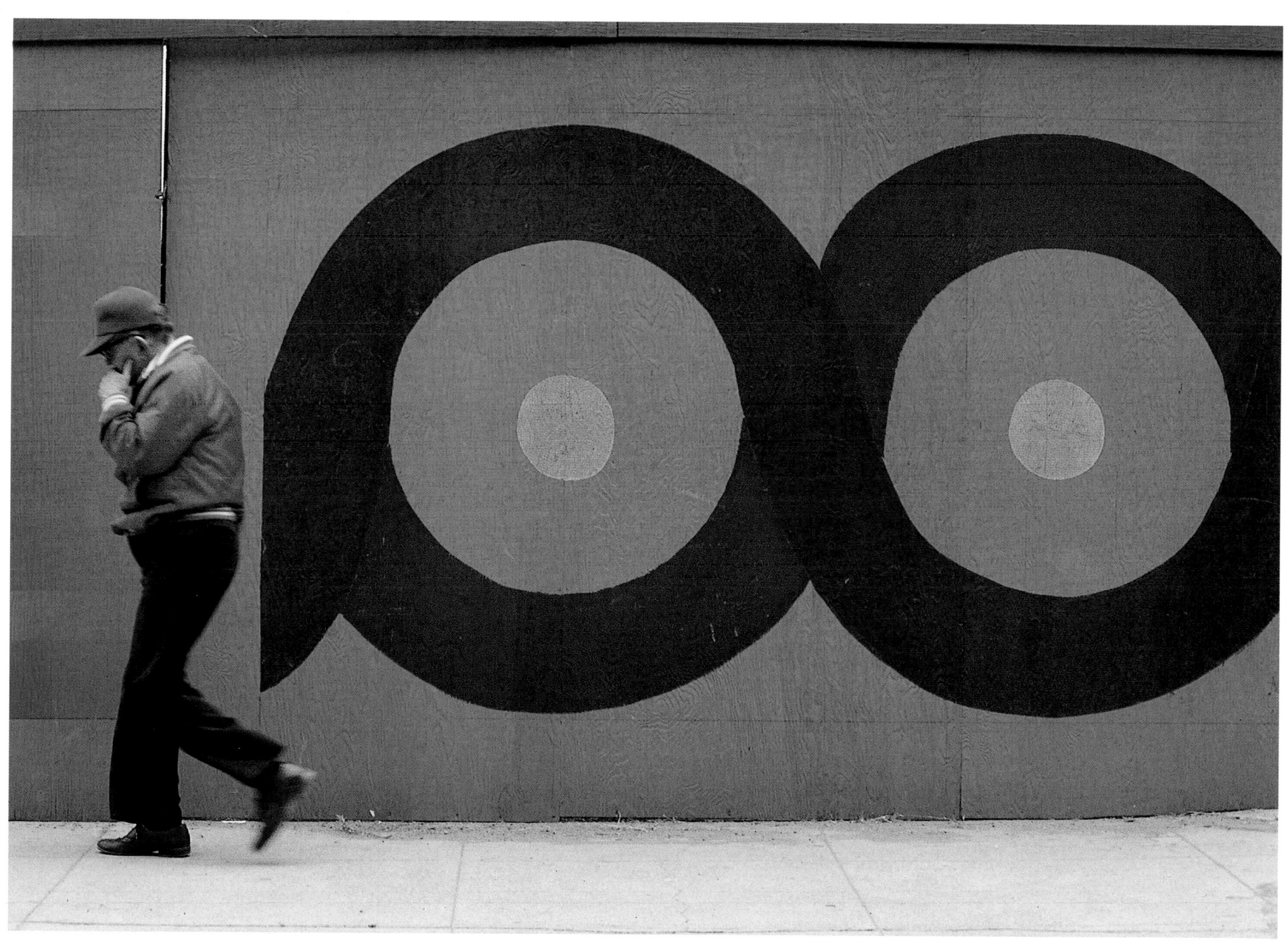

Painted wall 10th and Washington *June 1982*

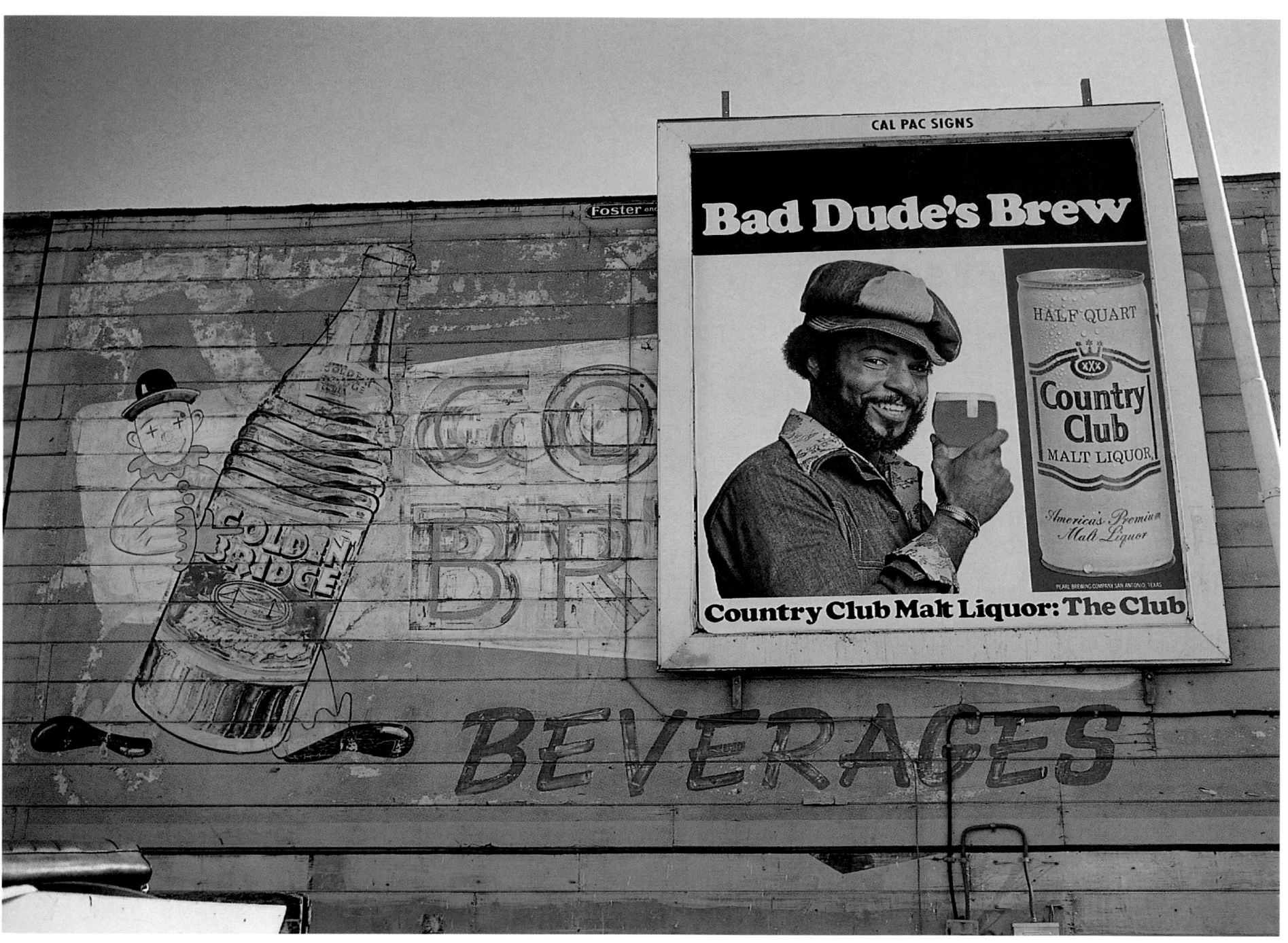

Bad Dude's Brew   7th near Jefferson   *May 1975*

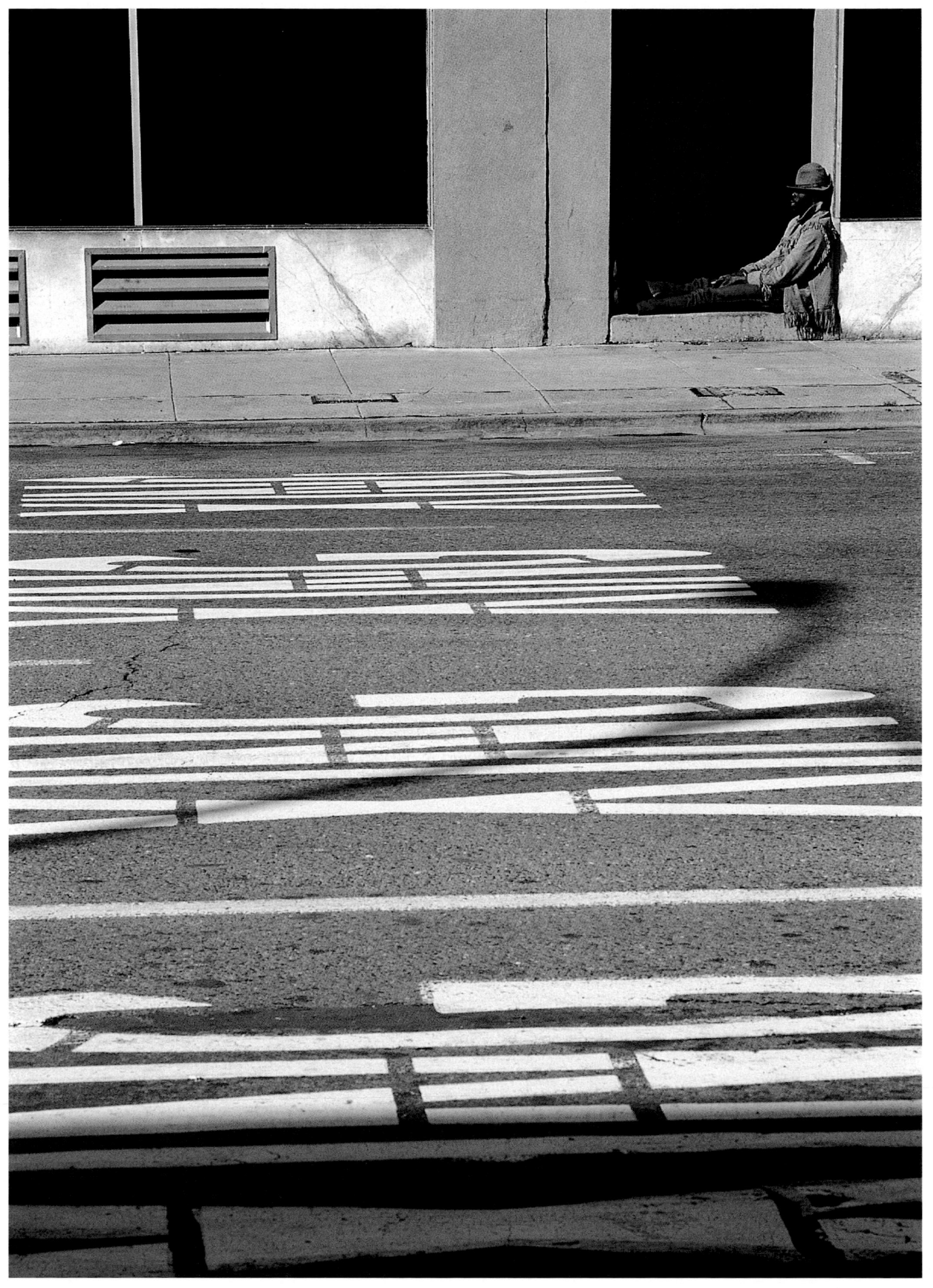

XING   10th near Jefferson   *April 1979*

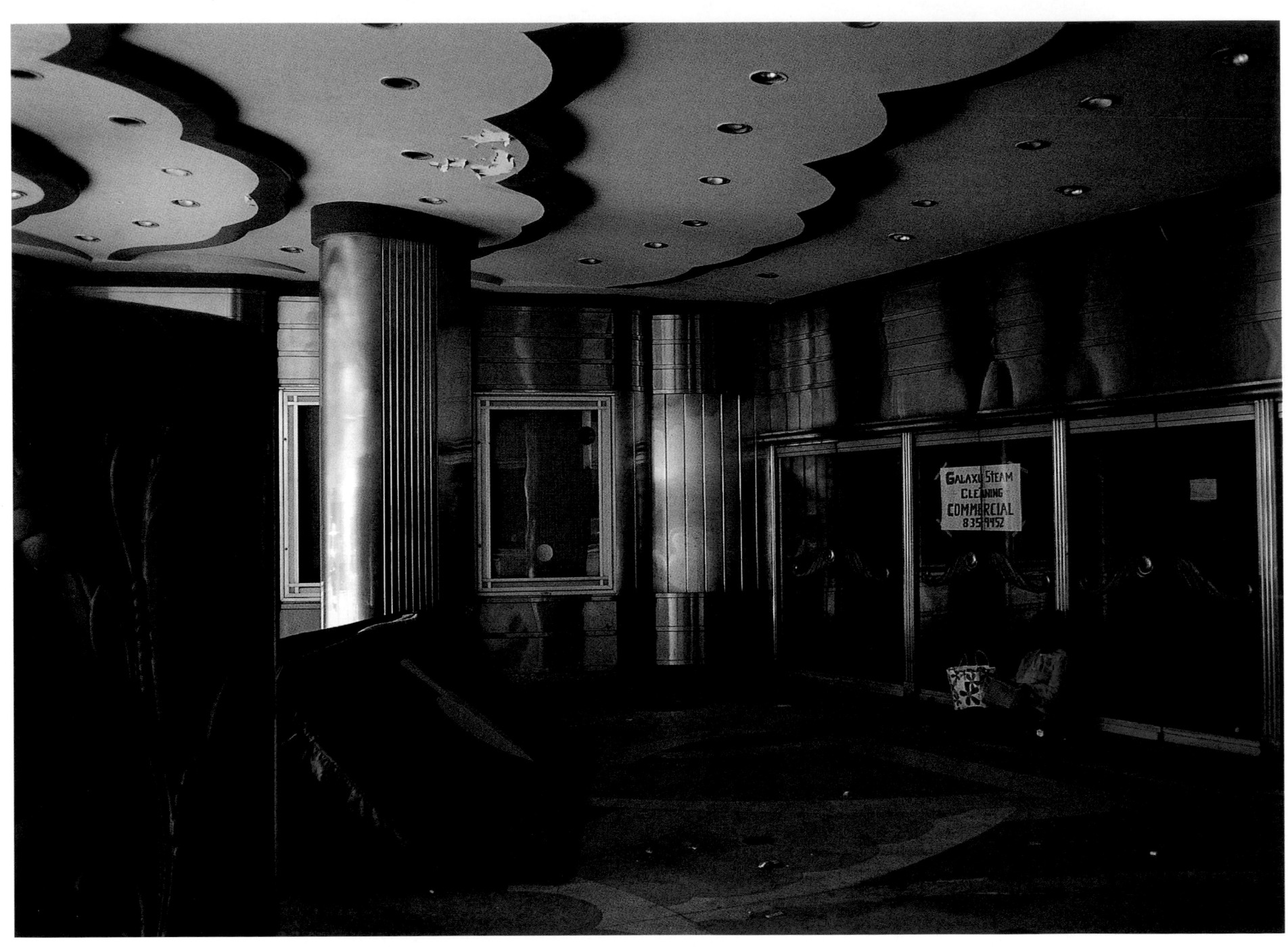

The Oakland Fox   Telegraph Avenue near 18th   *October 1980*

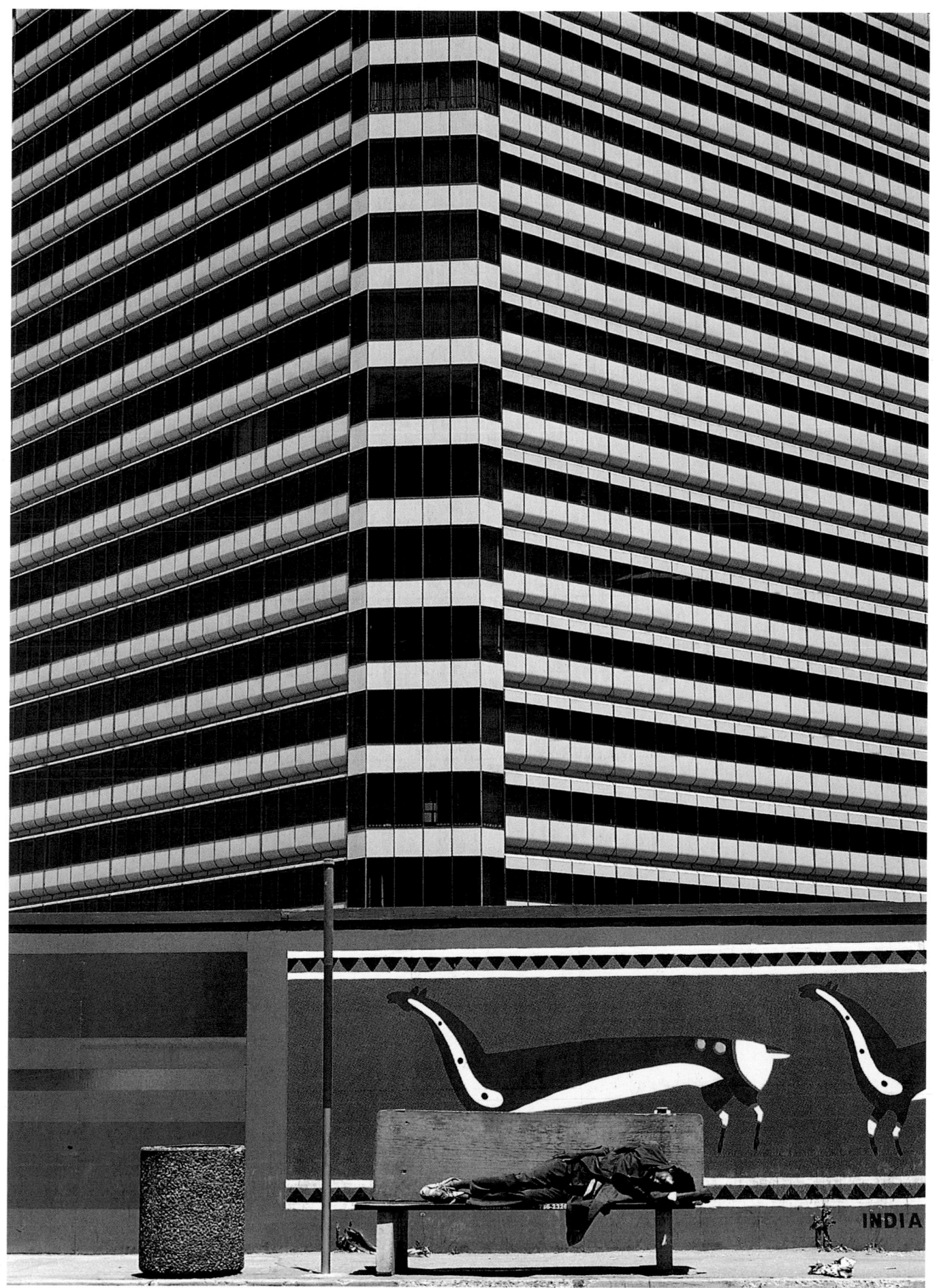

Still life 10th at Broadway *July 1982*

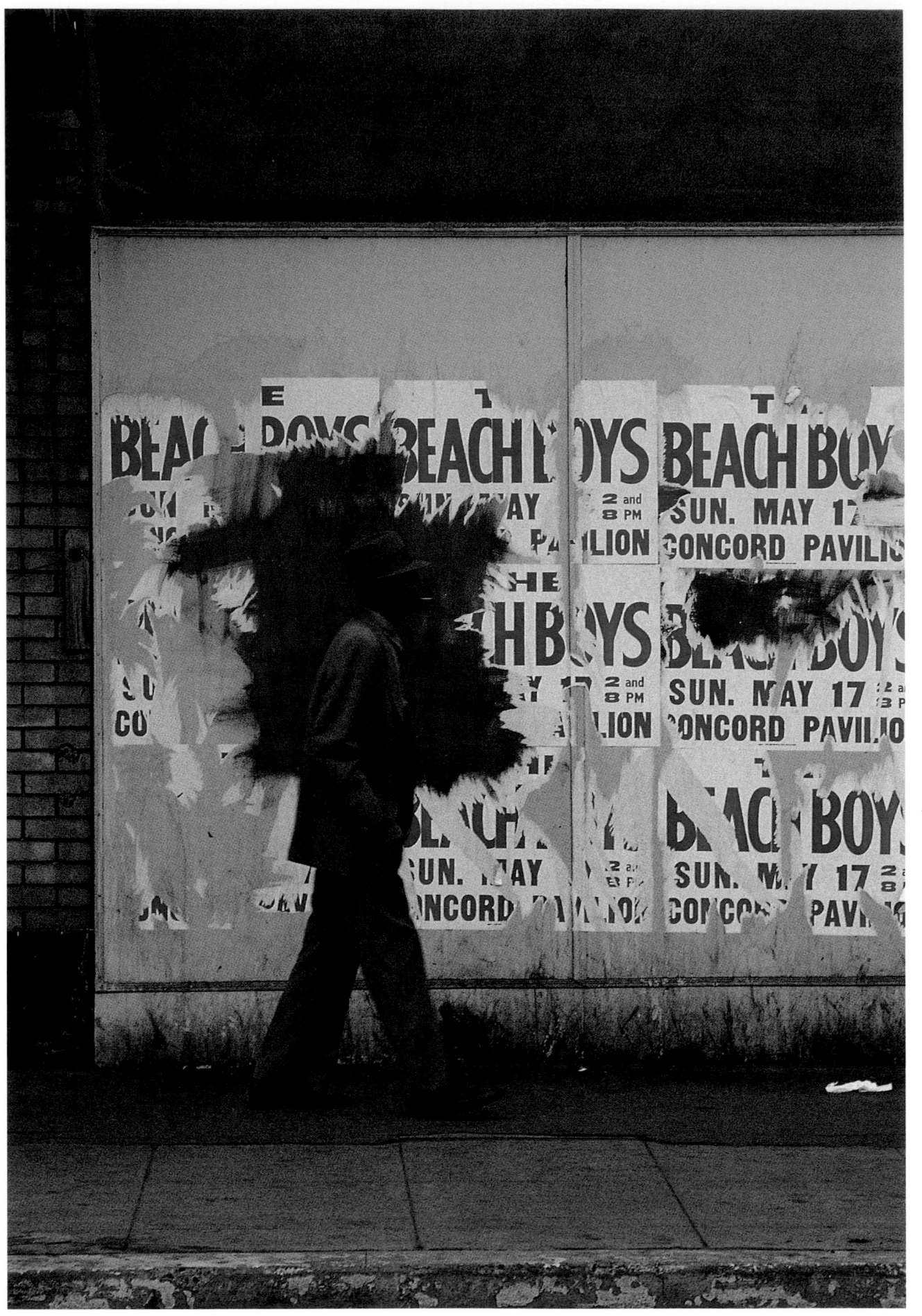

Beach Boys   10th and Washington   *November 1981*

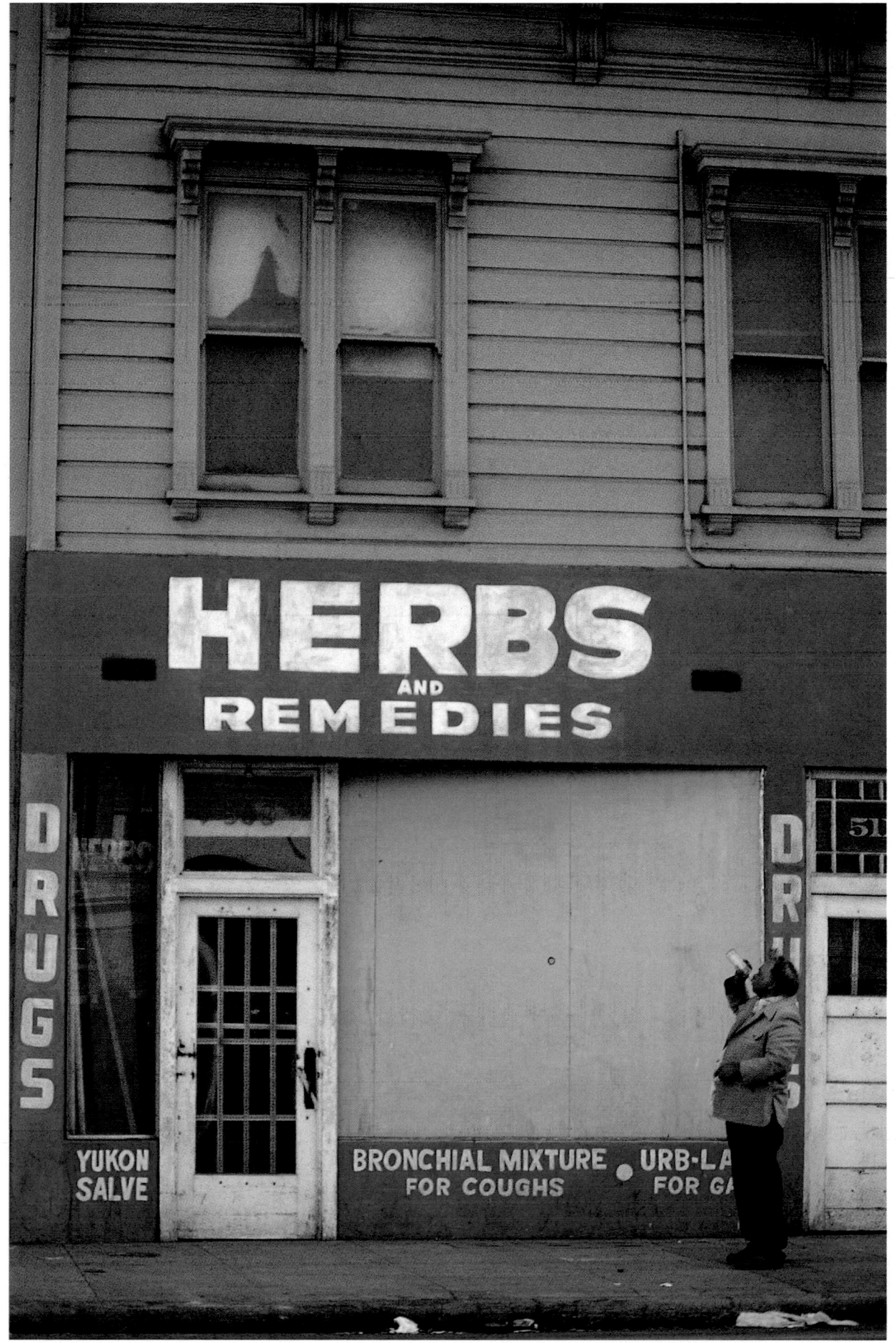

Herbs and Remedies   8th near Washington   *August 1982*

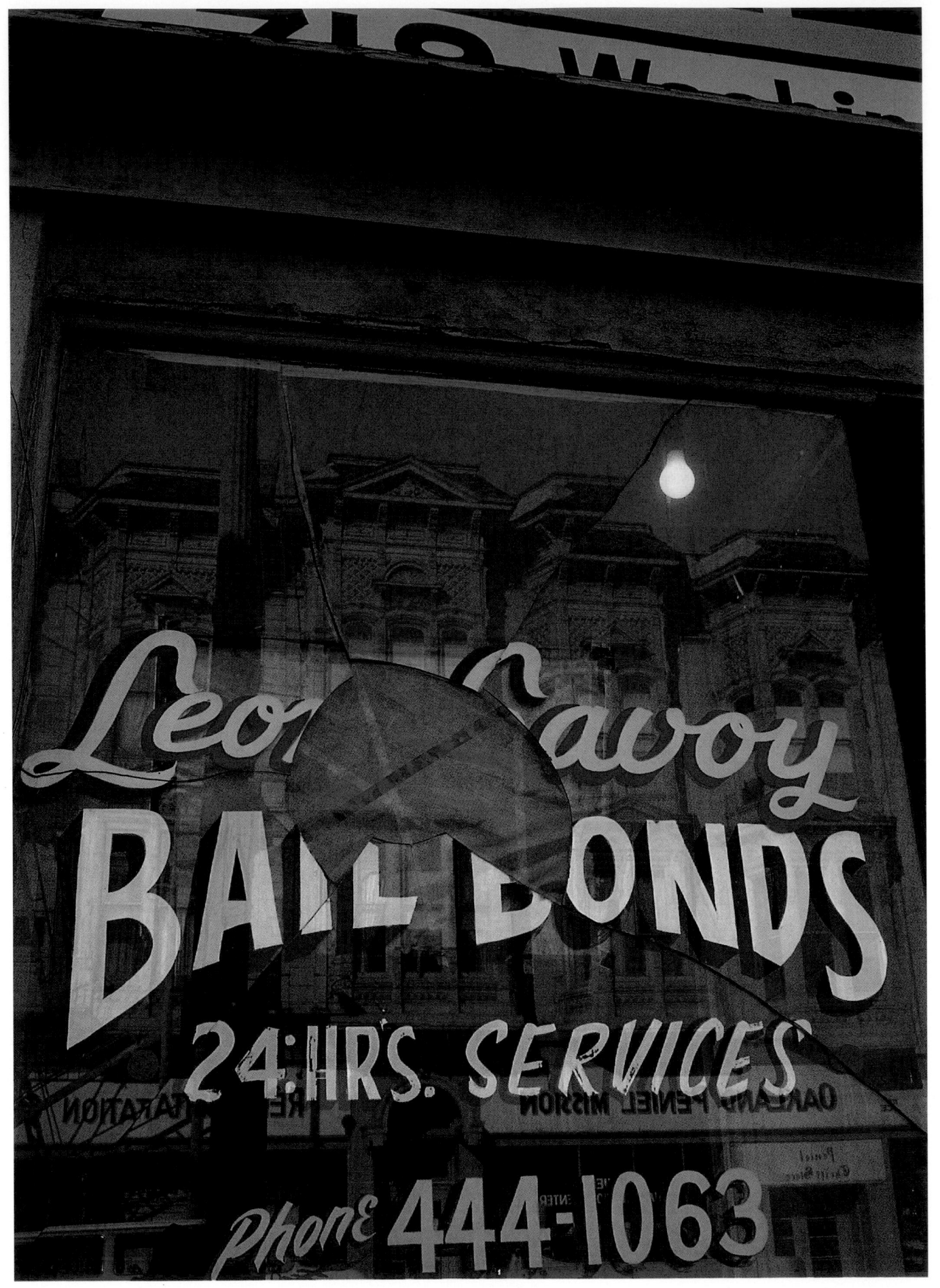

Bail Bonds   Washington and 8th   *April 1979*

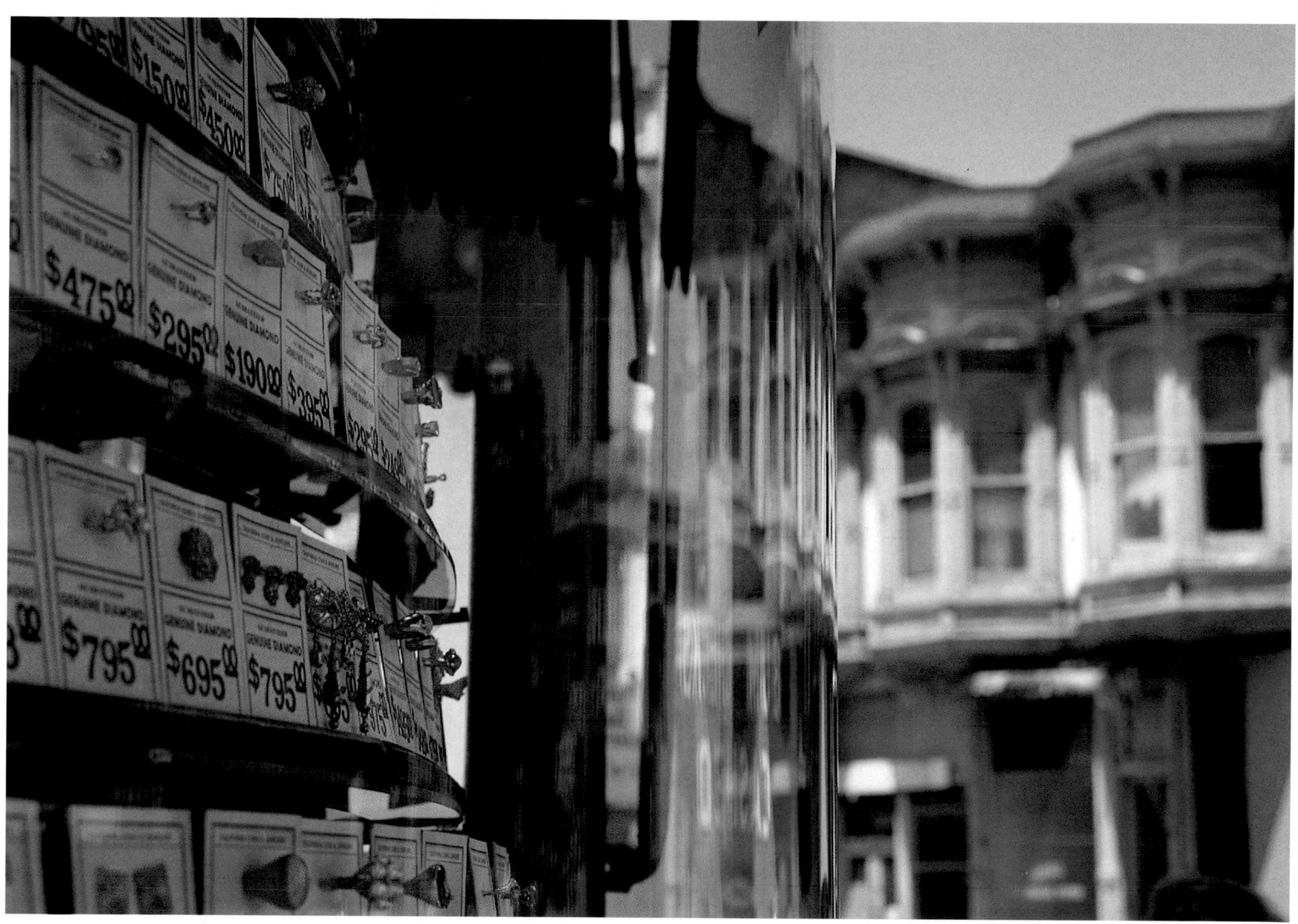

Precious jewels   9th at Broadway   *July 1982*

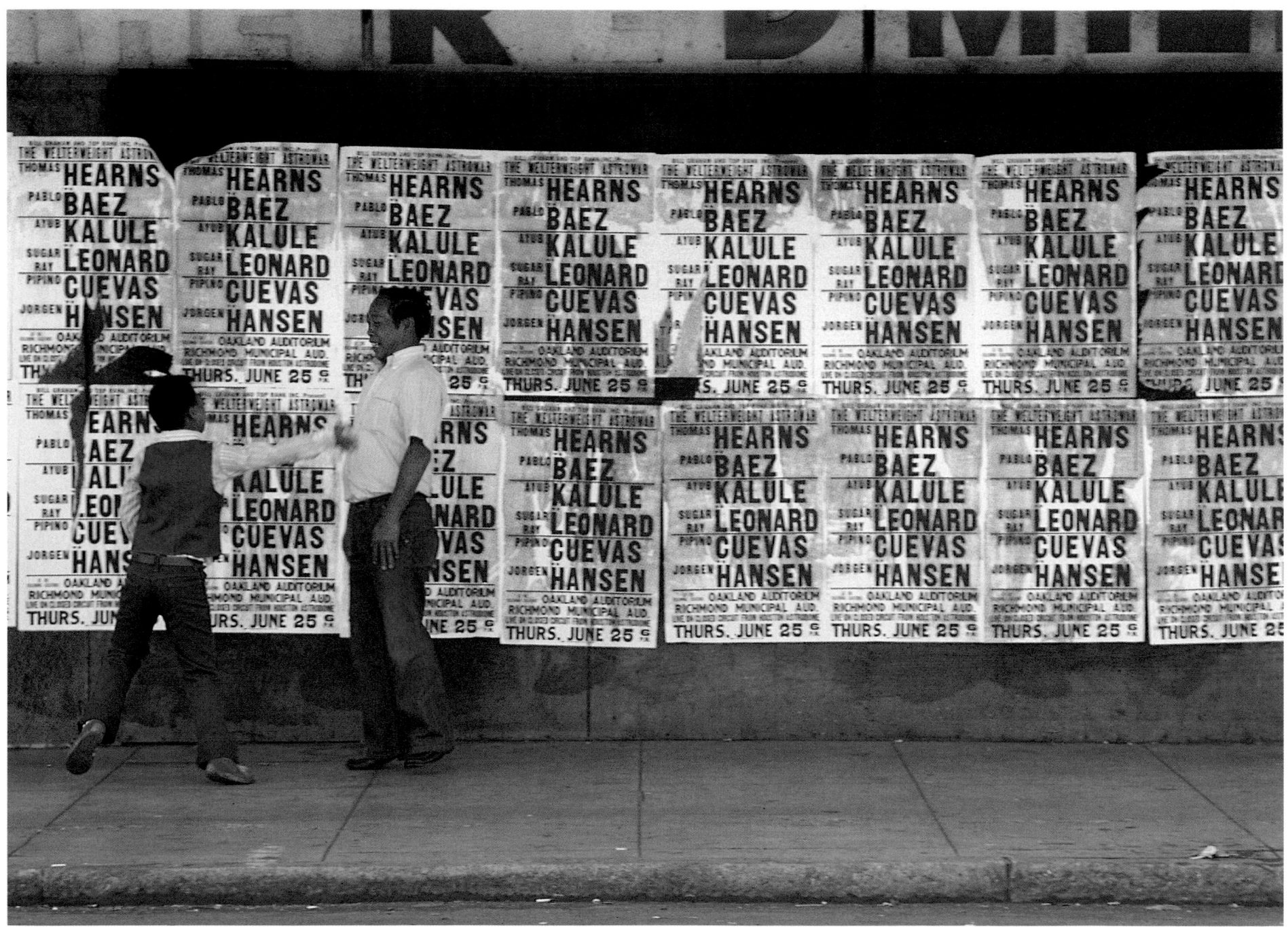

Boxing   8th near Washington   *July 1981*

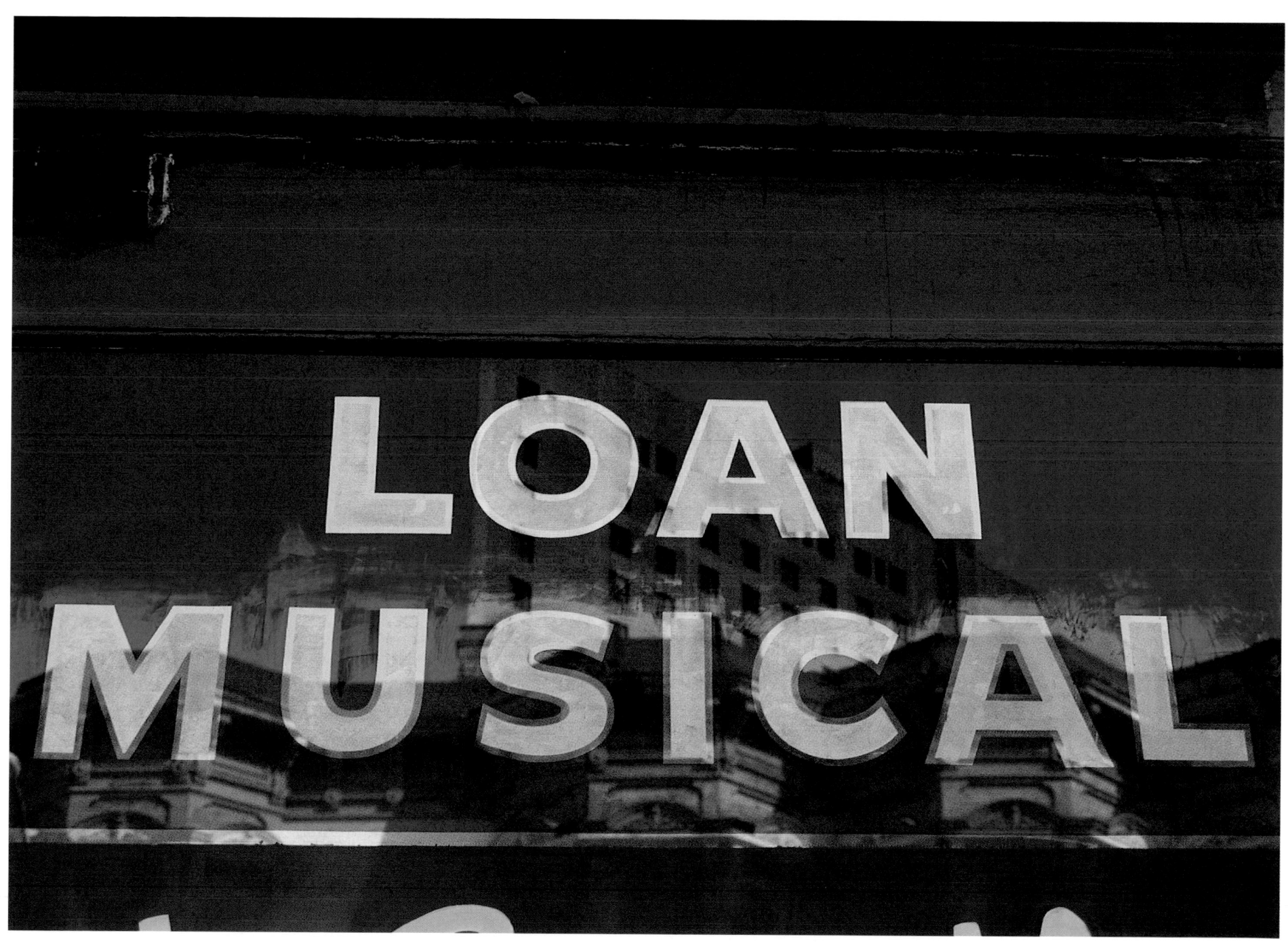

Loan/Musical   9th and Broadway   *May 1984*

SAN PABLO AVENUE

"Some Facts About A Street Which Was Originally A Country Road," begins an
article in the November 10, 1892 edition of the *Oakland Enquirer*, under the
headline, "A Long One."
The article details San Pablo Avenue's rich history. ". . . It is one of the longest straight
roads in the State, there not being a turn or a crook from Broadway out to San
Pablo town. It was built around 1856."

San Pablo Avenue has seen the Pony Express which used to arrive biweekly.
In those days the avenue hosted livery parlors and hotels with names like Hotel Del
Monte, Golden Gate. Coal oil businesses like H. P. Welcome and Co. . . .
A. A. Atkinson who specialized in pictures, frames and mirrors . . . Howell's Drug
Store which boasted "a new stock of perfumeries, colognes, and toilet articles to
satisfy the most refined aesthetic tastes." The newspaper said that next to Broadway,
San Pablo Avenue had the brightest future of any of Oakland's thoroughfares.

All of that is gone now.
A faded memory symbolized by a sign on a brick wall,
"Owl Cigars, now 5 cents." Here and there only a reminder of the former glory. Like
Nagler's photo of brown hands in the window, the contemporary San Pablo Avenue
doesn't seem to have a prayer. A series of cheap rooming houses and bars belie the
optimism of a hundred years ago. Contemporary San Pablo Avenue is a skid row . . . a
drug and alcohol market.

A man swallows his pride and peddles trash to make ends meet. "Basic Pleasure" and
"Basic Pain" says the sign in the background. His basic pleasure is a cigarette. The
symbol of tragedy in Oakland these days is an abandoned shopping cart with all of
one's belongings inside the basket. Another soul has reached rock bottom. Fallen
through the safety net.

— Ishmael Reed

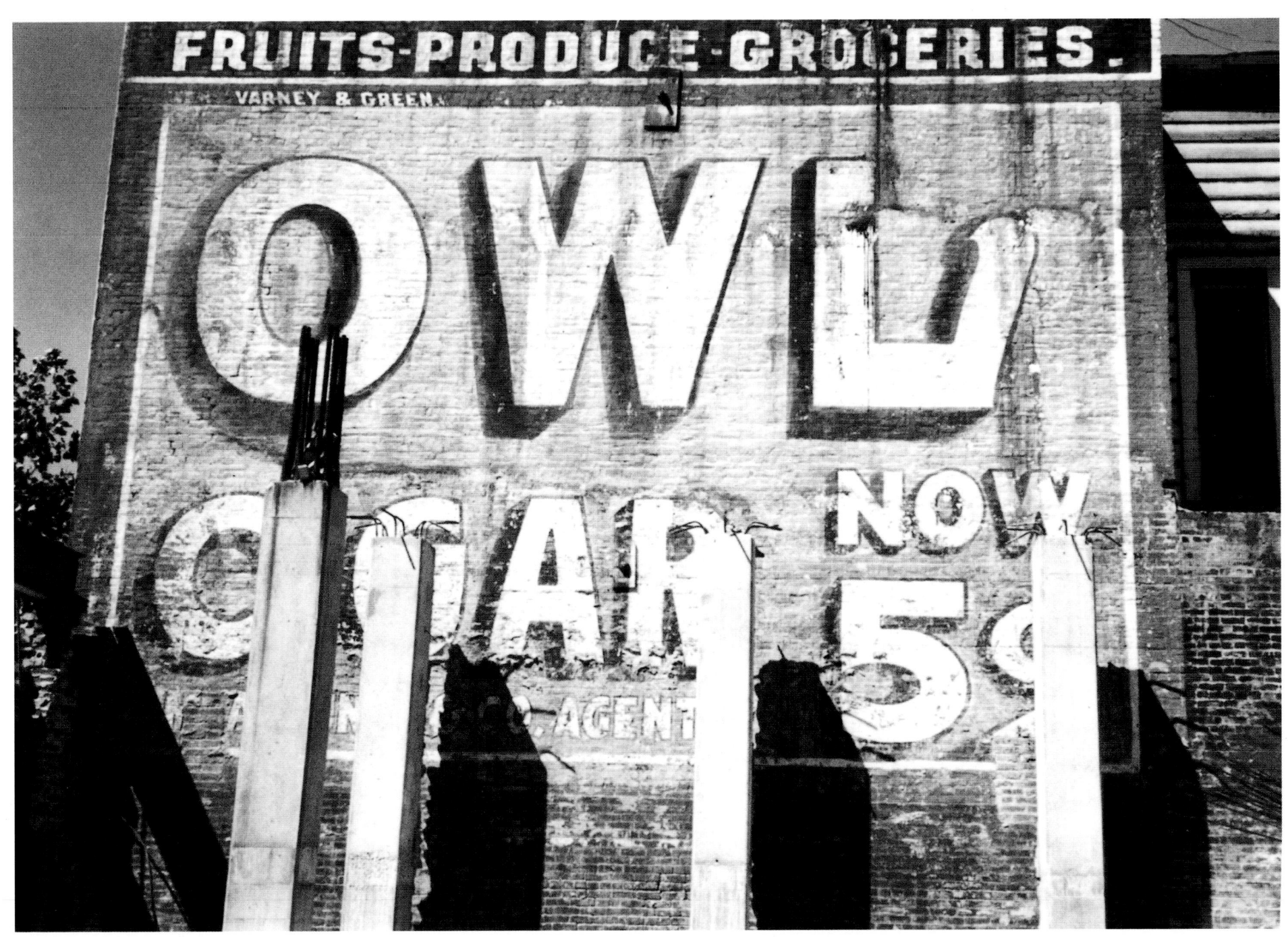

Owl Cigars   18th and San Pablo Avenue   *November 1989*

41.

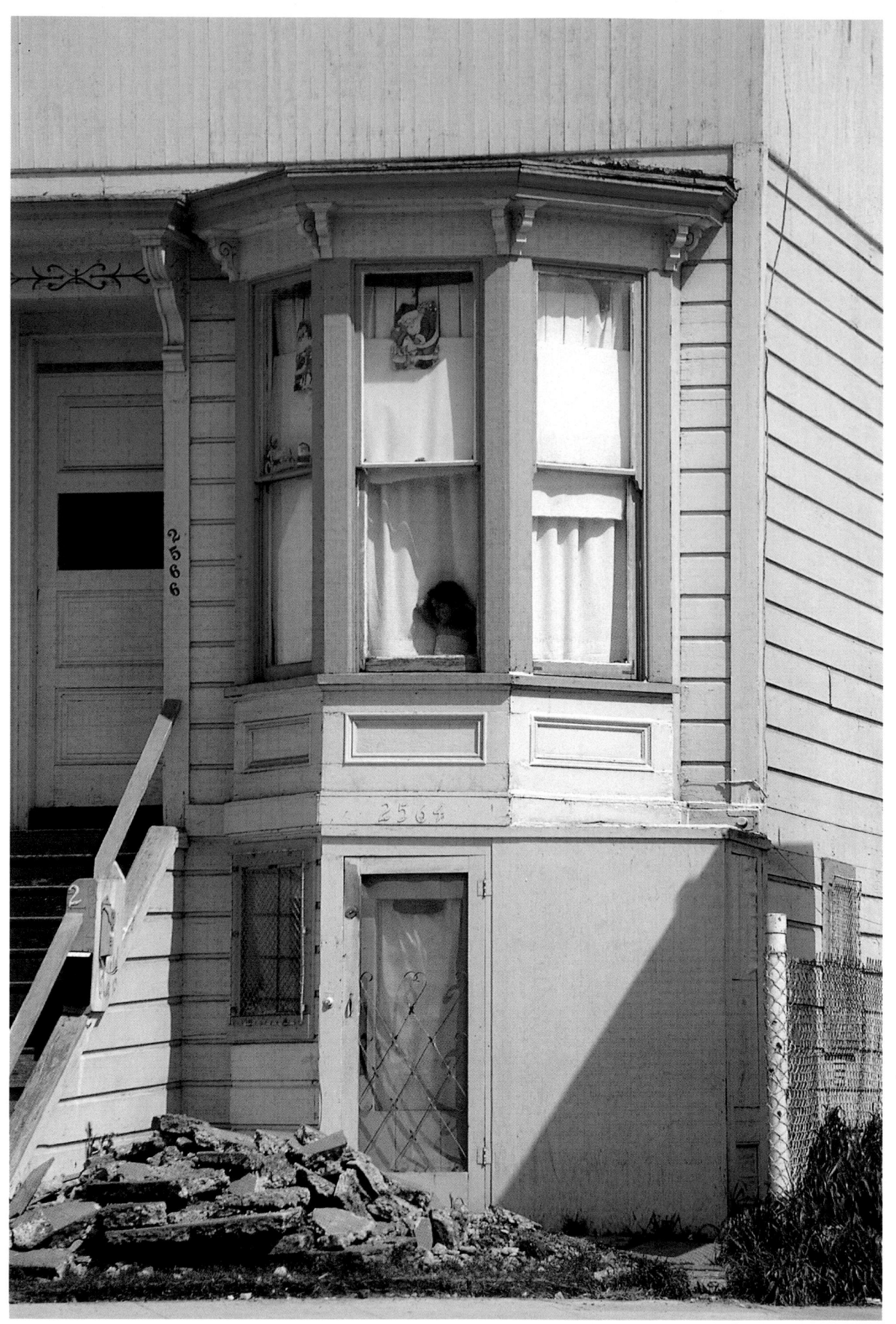

Girl in window   San Pablo Avenue near 27th   *April 1983*

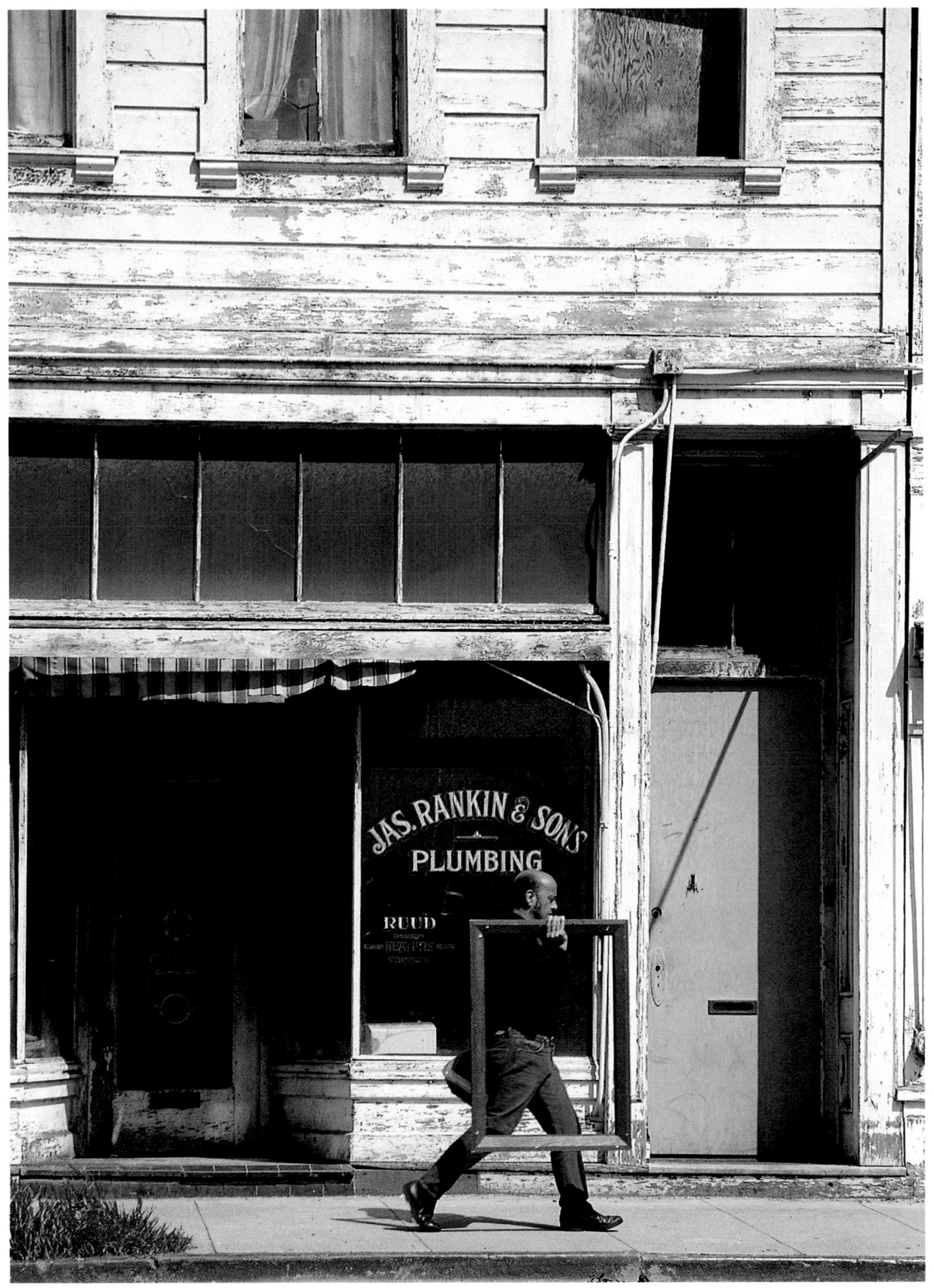

Framed   18th and San Pablo Avenue   *April 1983*

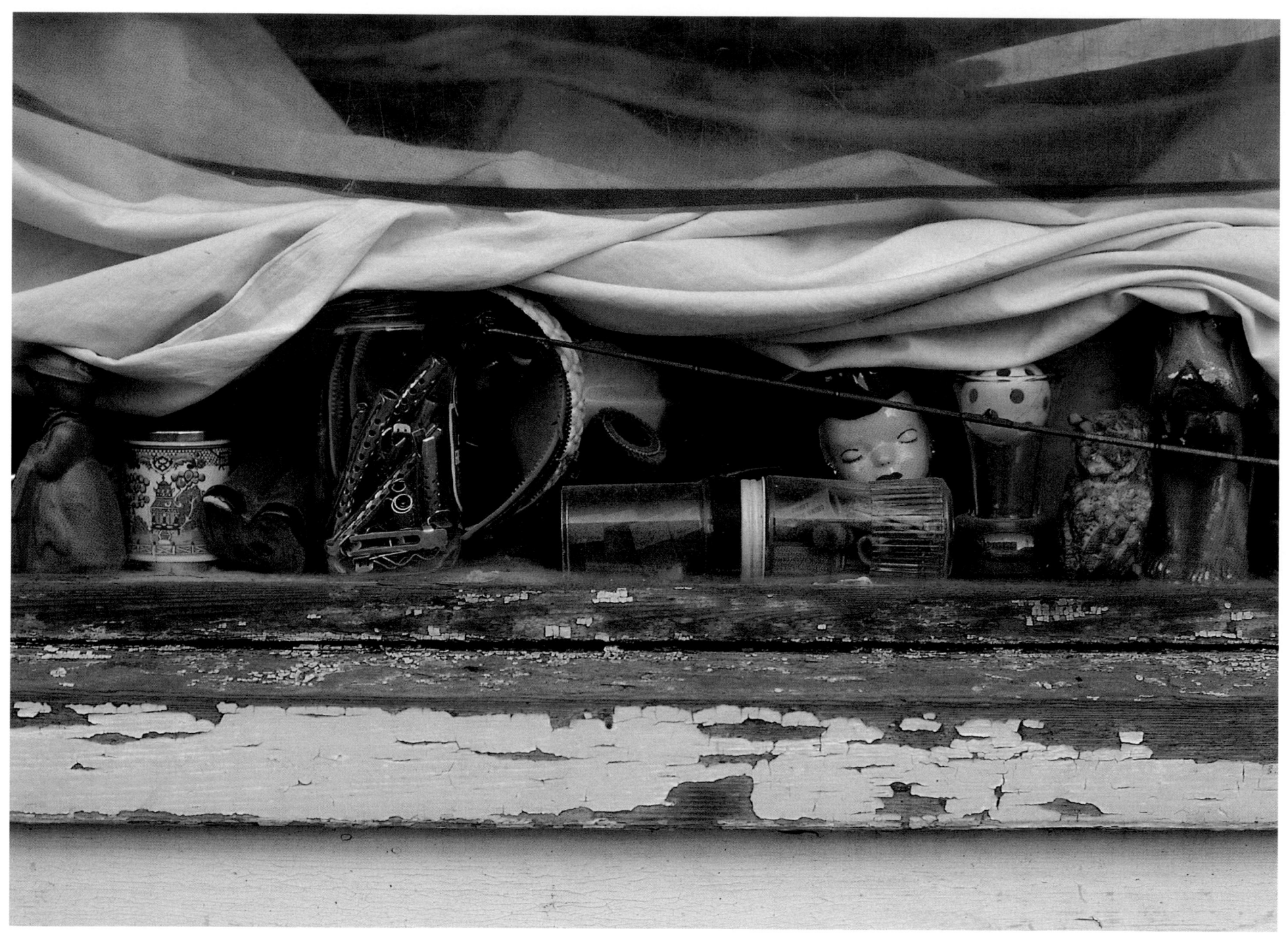

Junk Store window   20th and San Pablo Avenue   *September 1976*

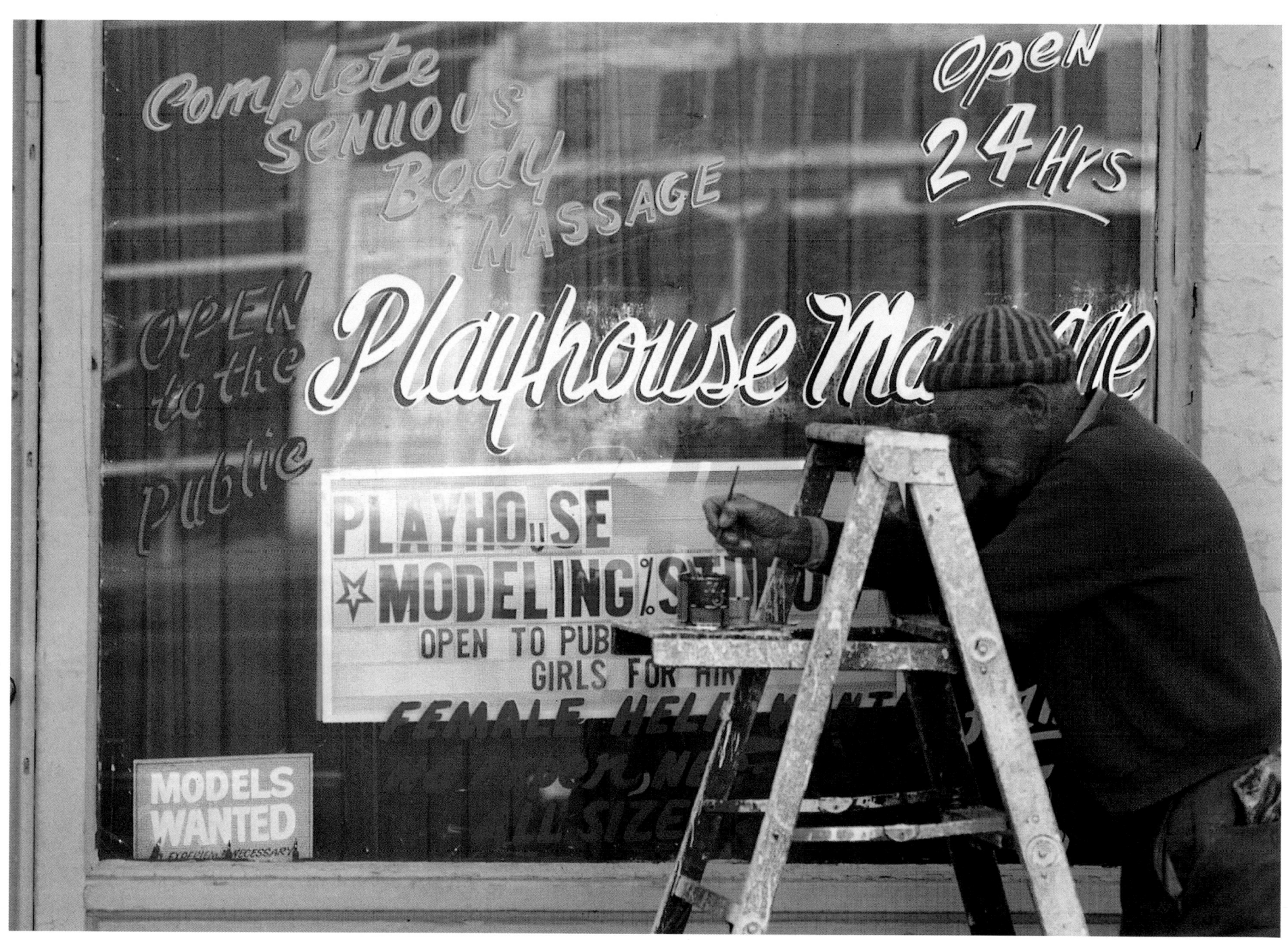

Artist at work   20th and San Pablo Avenue   *March 1977*

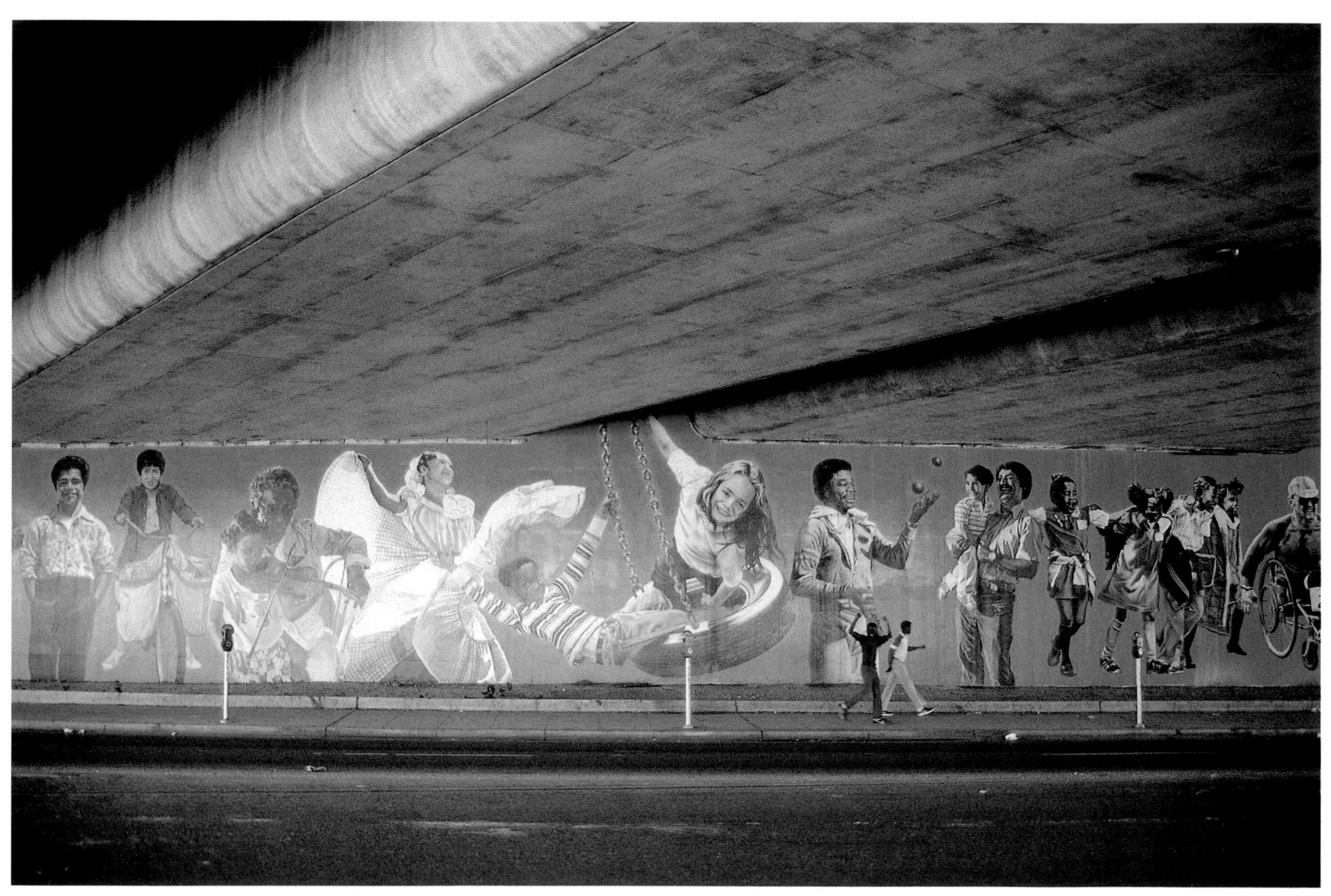

Mural   San Pablo Avenue near 20th   *March 1984*

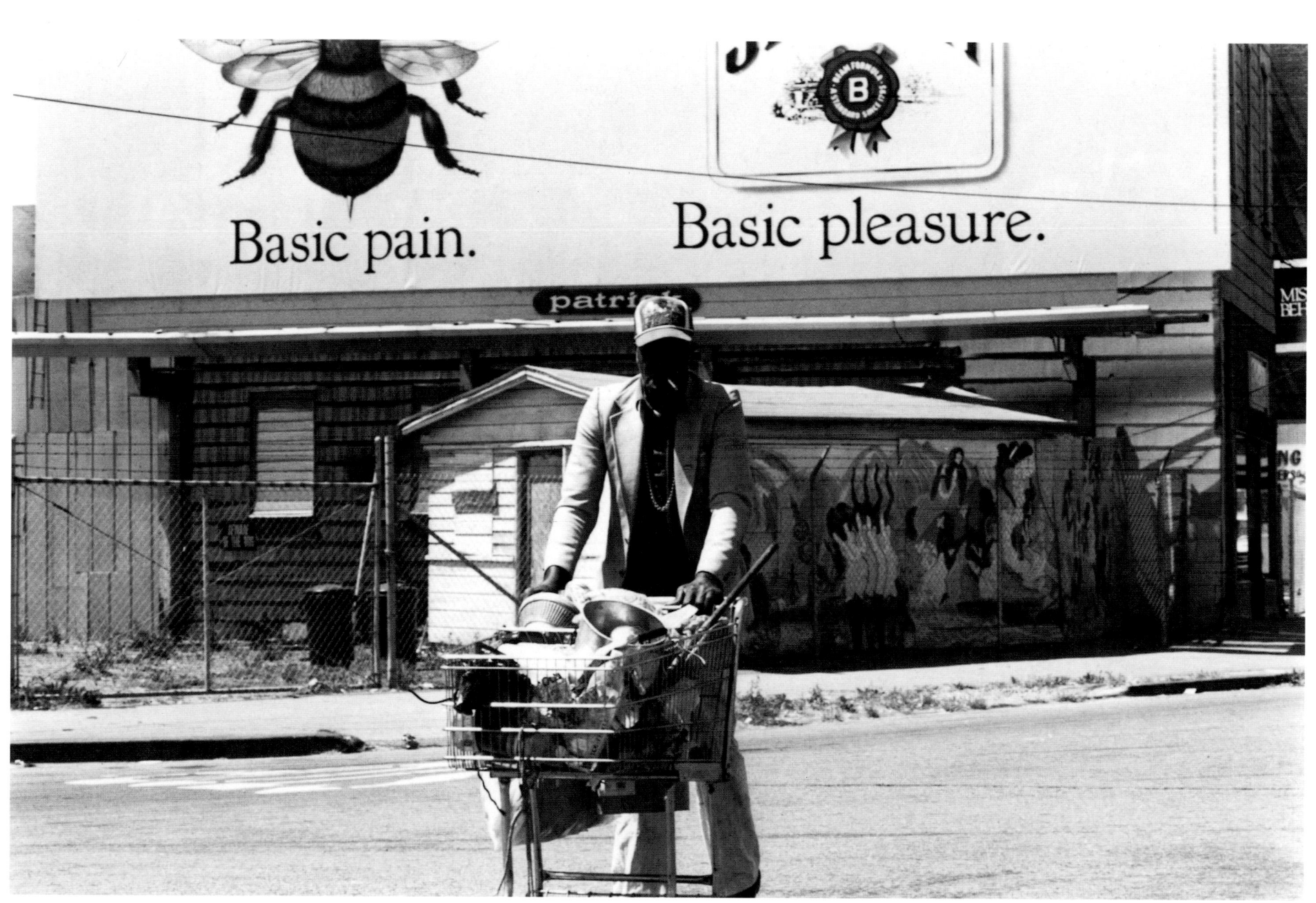

Basic pain/Basic pleasure   35th and San Pablo Avenue   *July 1992*

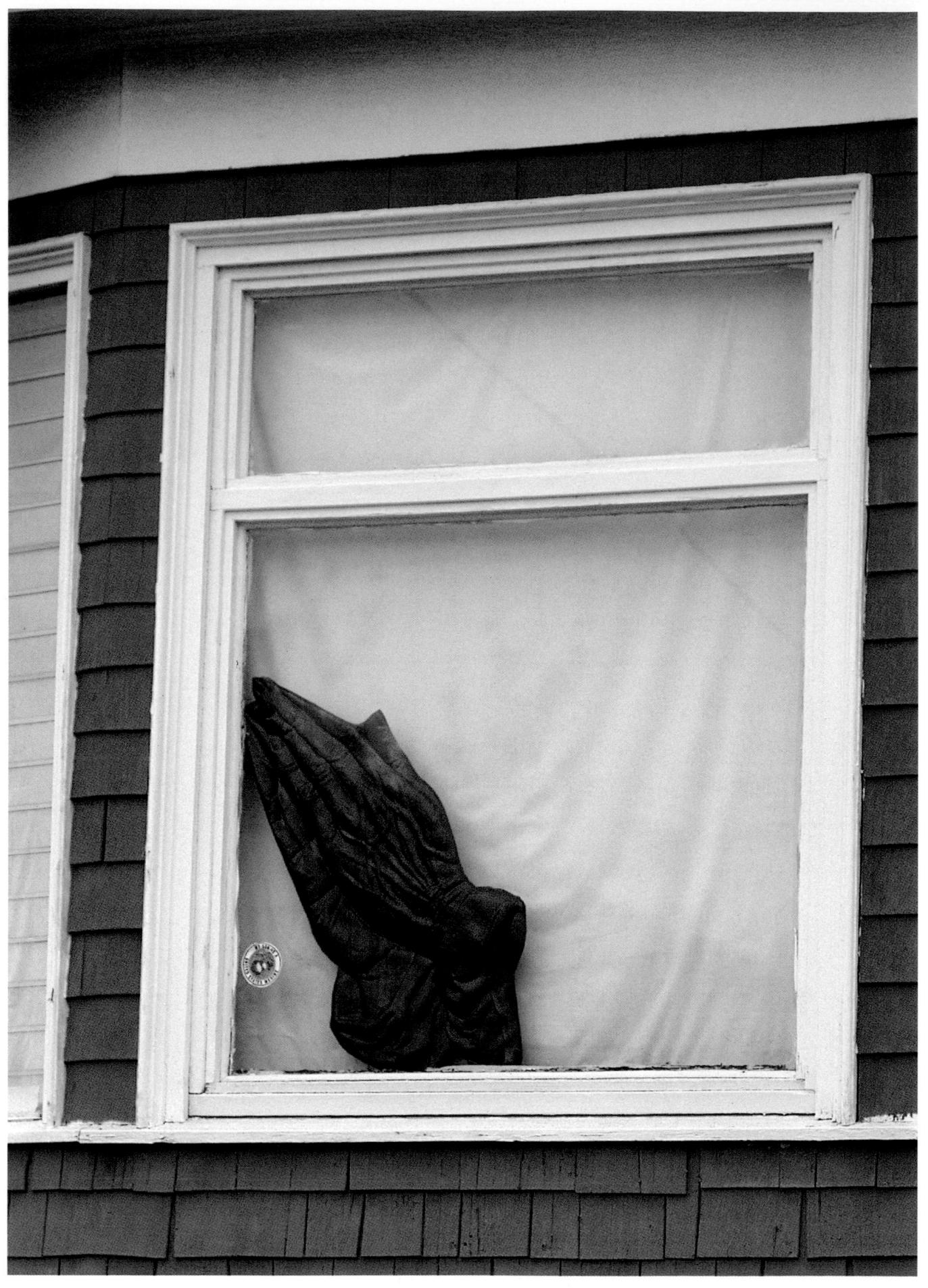

Hands in prayer   San Pablo Avenue near 27th   *May 1975*

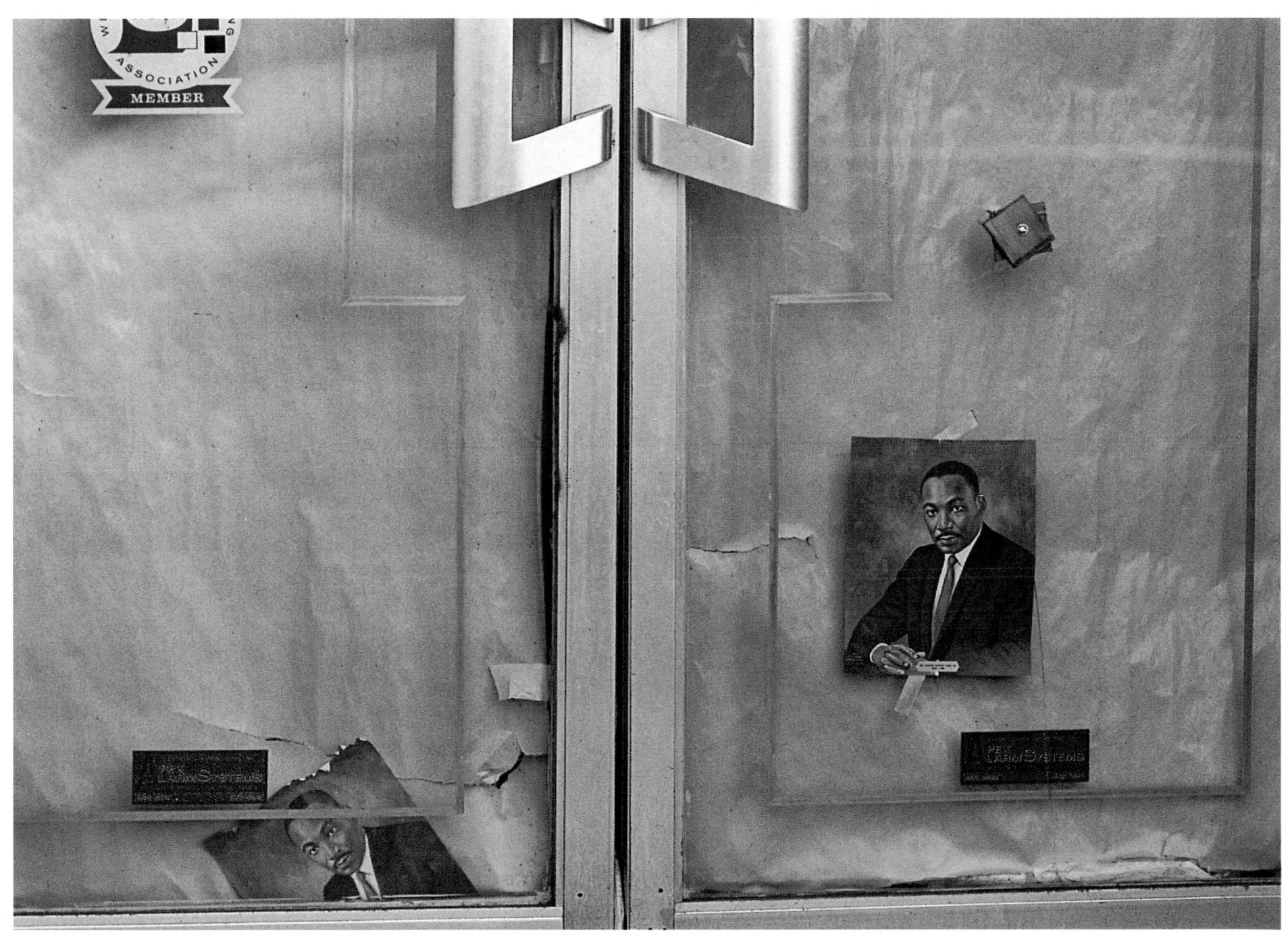

Martin Luther King   18th and San Pablo Avenue   *February 1976*

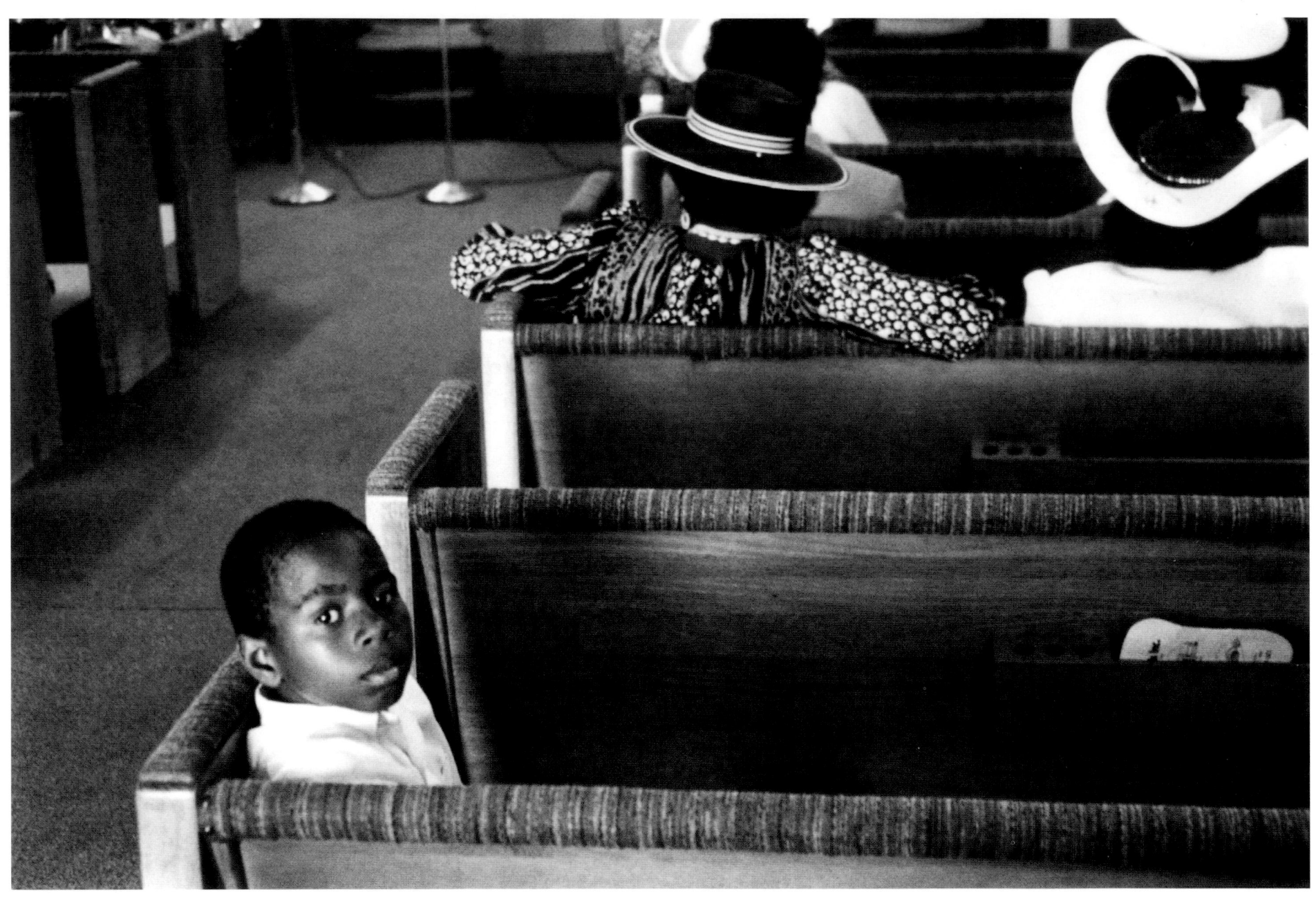

Easter Sunday   San Pablo Avenue   *April 1990*

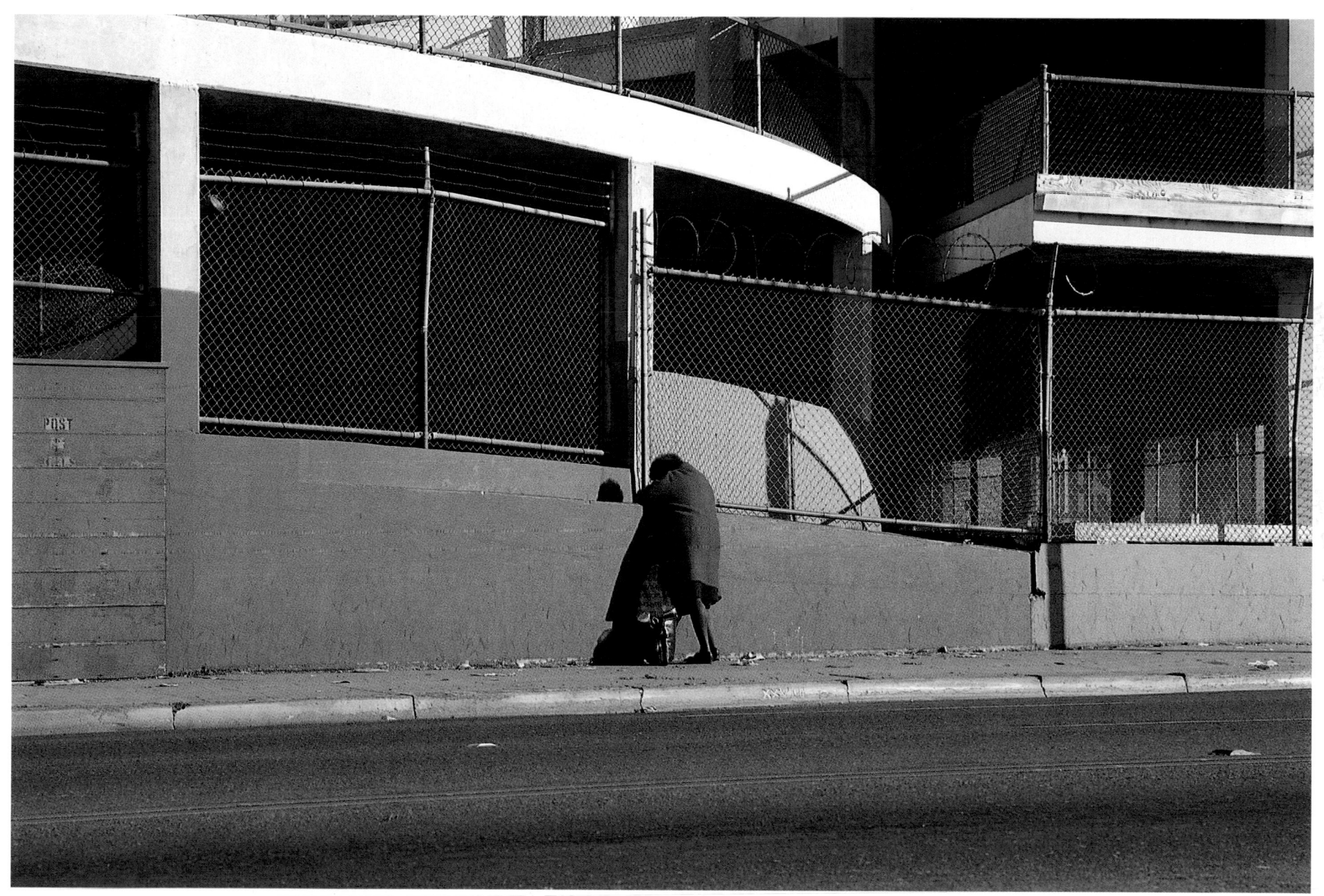

Woman at a bus stop   19th and San Pablo Avenue   *January 1982*

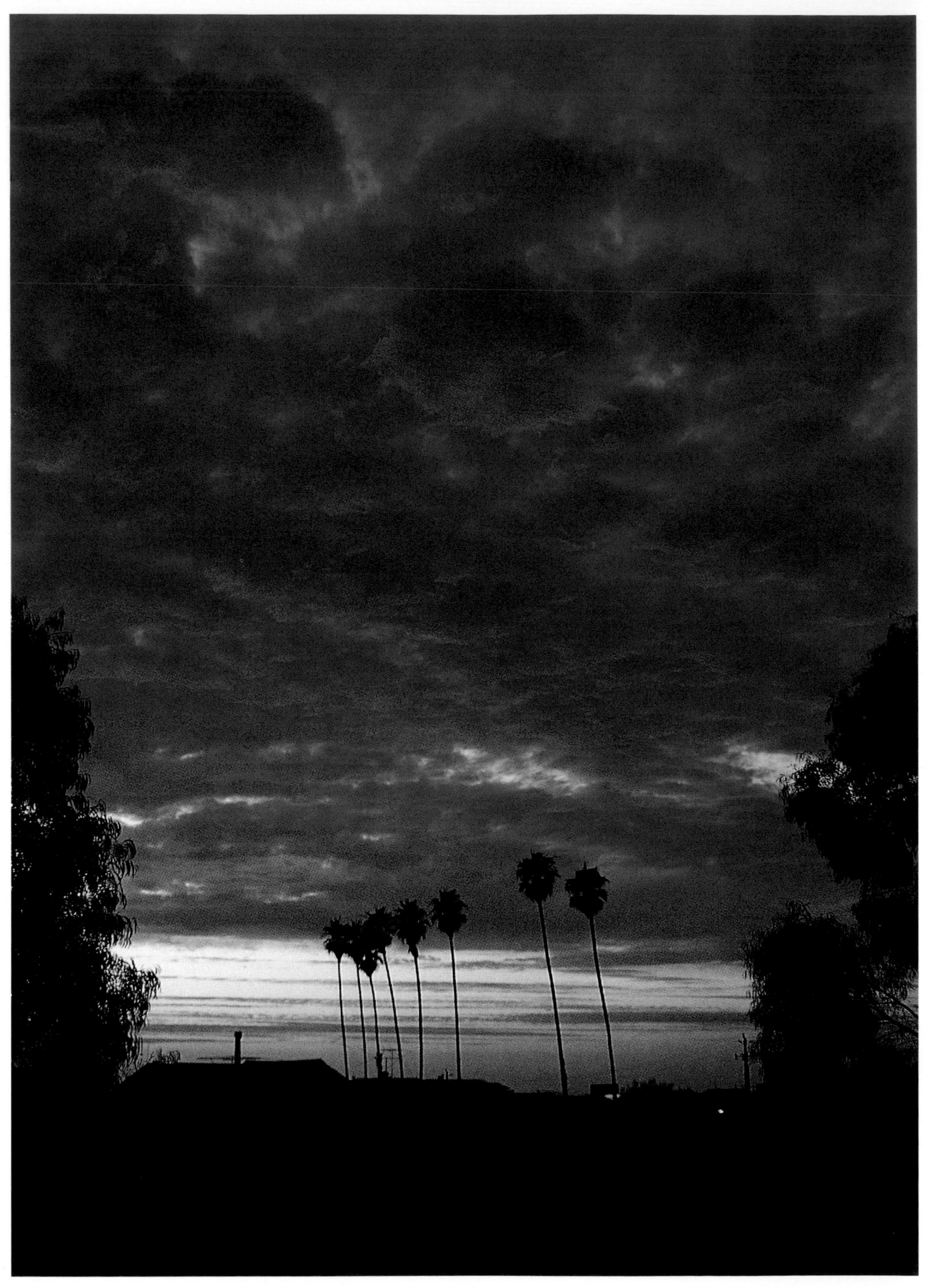

Sunset   San Pablo Avenue near 25th   *August 1982*

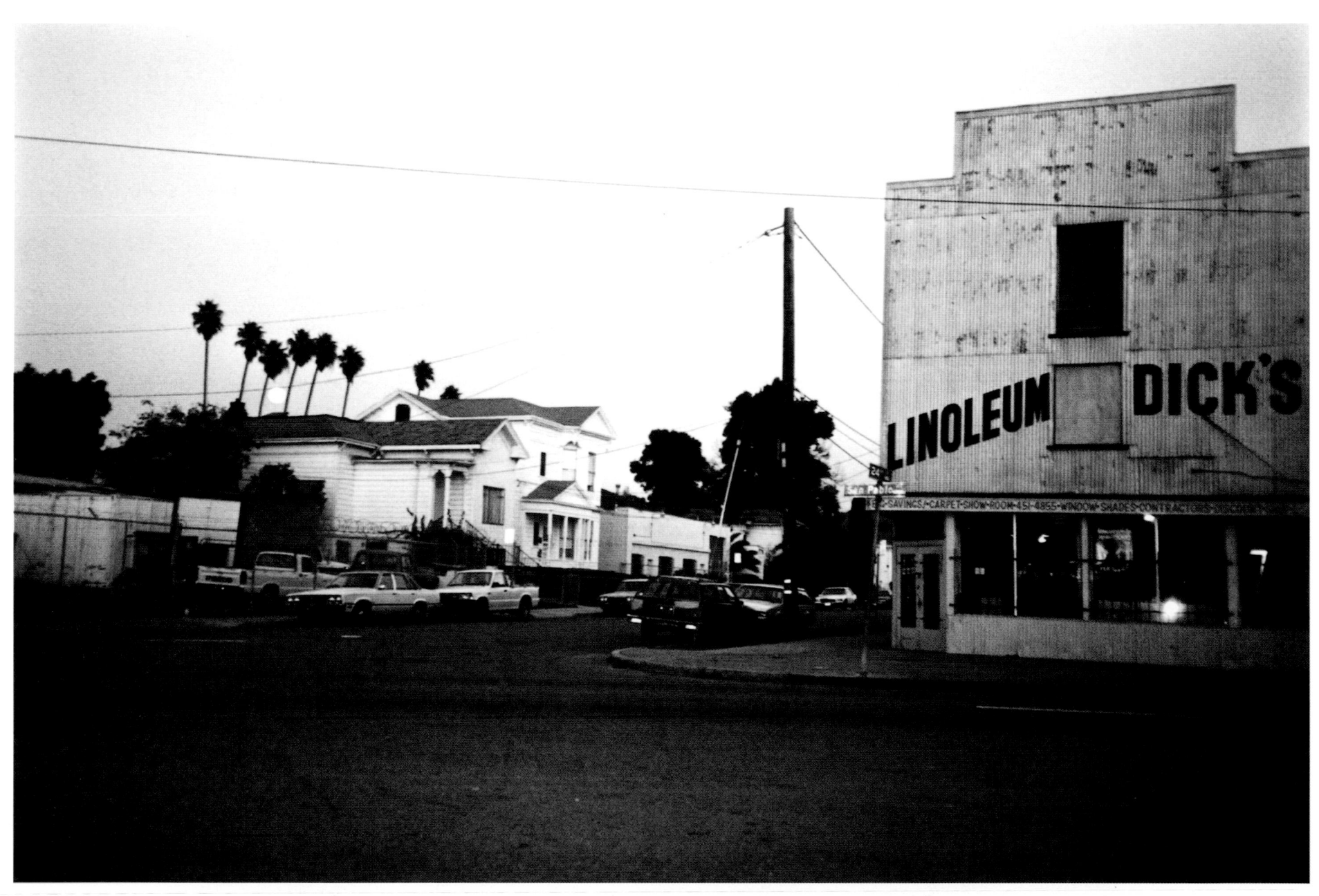

Moonrise on San Pablo   24th and San Pablo Avenue   *November 1990*

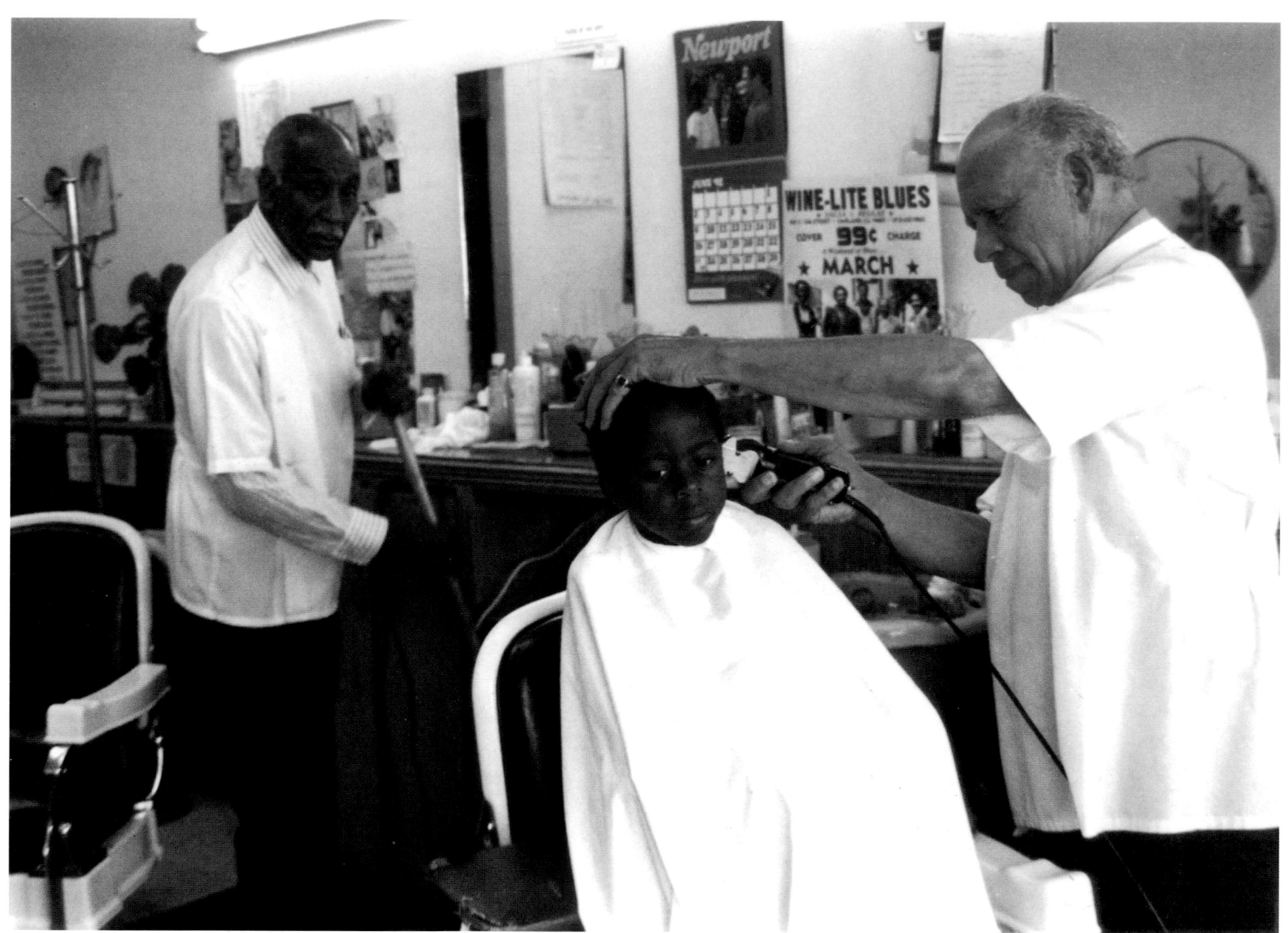

Haircut   San Pablo Avenue near 30th   *June 1992*

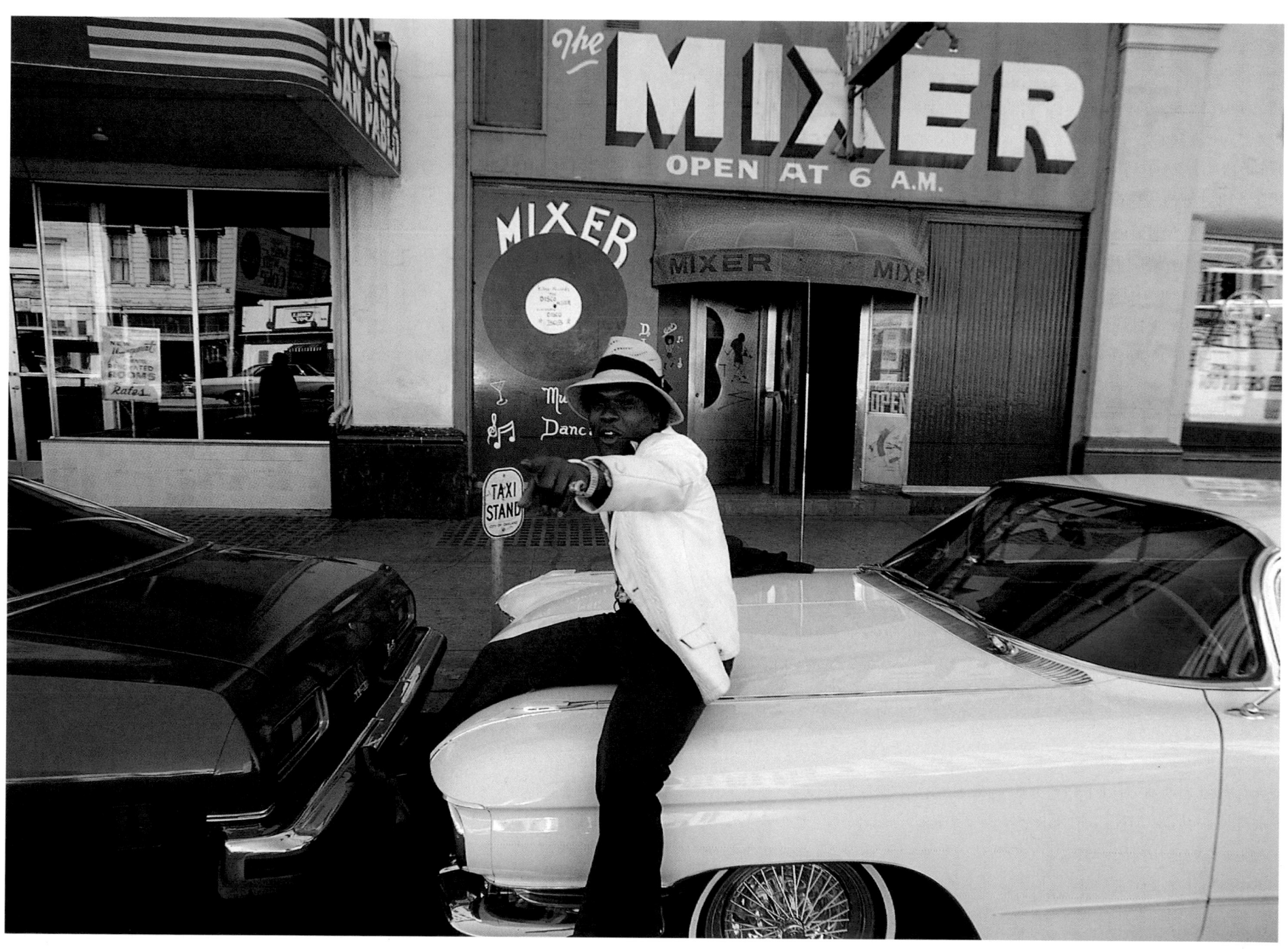

Hotel San Pablo   San Pablo Avenue near 20th   *May 1978*

A FEW WORDS ABOUT OAKLAND

Though a picture is worth a thousand words, words help.
Otherwise, why would painters and photographers accompany their visual products
    with words? Sometimes the words are better known than the picture — "found"
    words matched with the photo's subjects can say more than the editorials.
A working class everyman sits, separated from a building with an imposing
    AMERICA written on its wall. This shows the alienation of the worker from the
    system as well as Clifford Odets.

The spirit of the past coheres with the cheap facades of the present. The ghostly image
    of a gray-haired black woman peeps from behind the second story of a window.
    The sign says, "Time." Someone has written "Lies" in big letters on a blue wall
    before which a black man dressed in judgment-black walks, his hands behind his
    back. A shadow seems to be pointing to the letters. It is the finger of God, perhaps.

Langston Hughes said that a dream deferred becomes dried up like a raisin in the sun.
This idea is captured in Nagler's portrait of a young black girl, attired in bright
    accessories, while behind her is a storefront, on which the word "faith" is spelled
    backwards.

How long will it be before her faith crumbles?

— *Ishmael Reed*

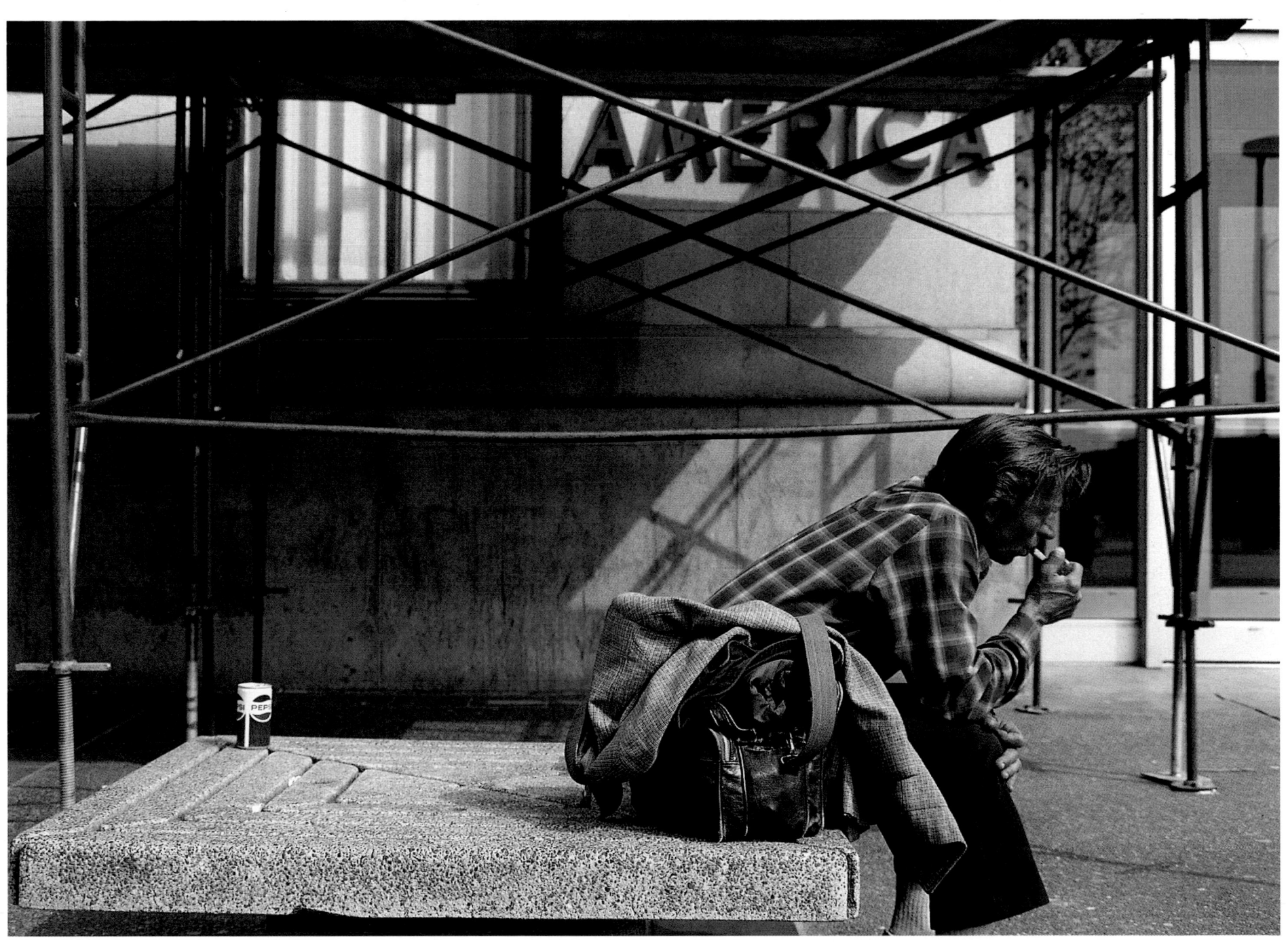

America   12th and Broadway   *April 1983*

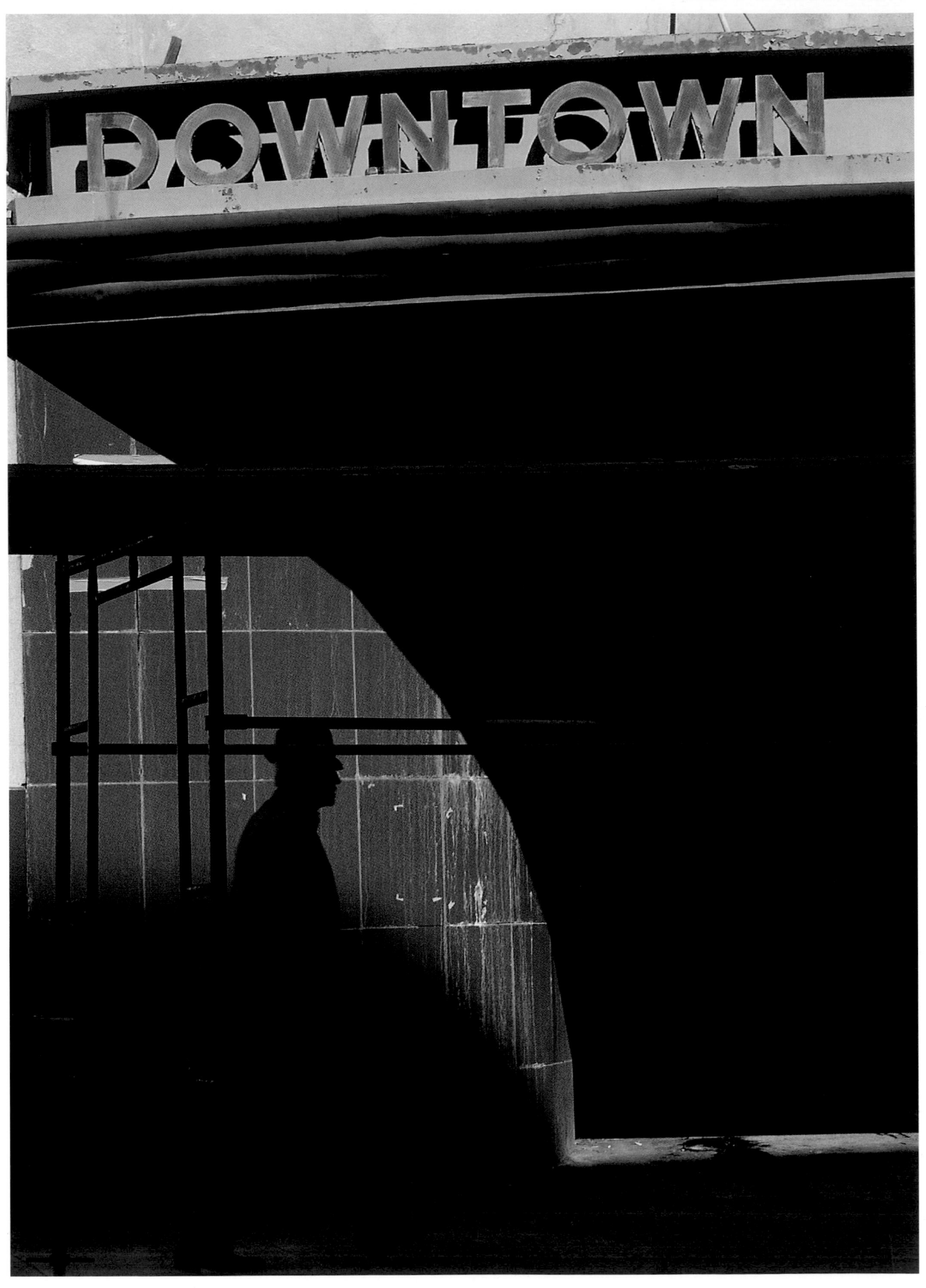

Downtown   10th near Washington   *March 1981*

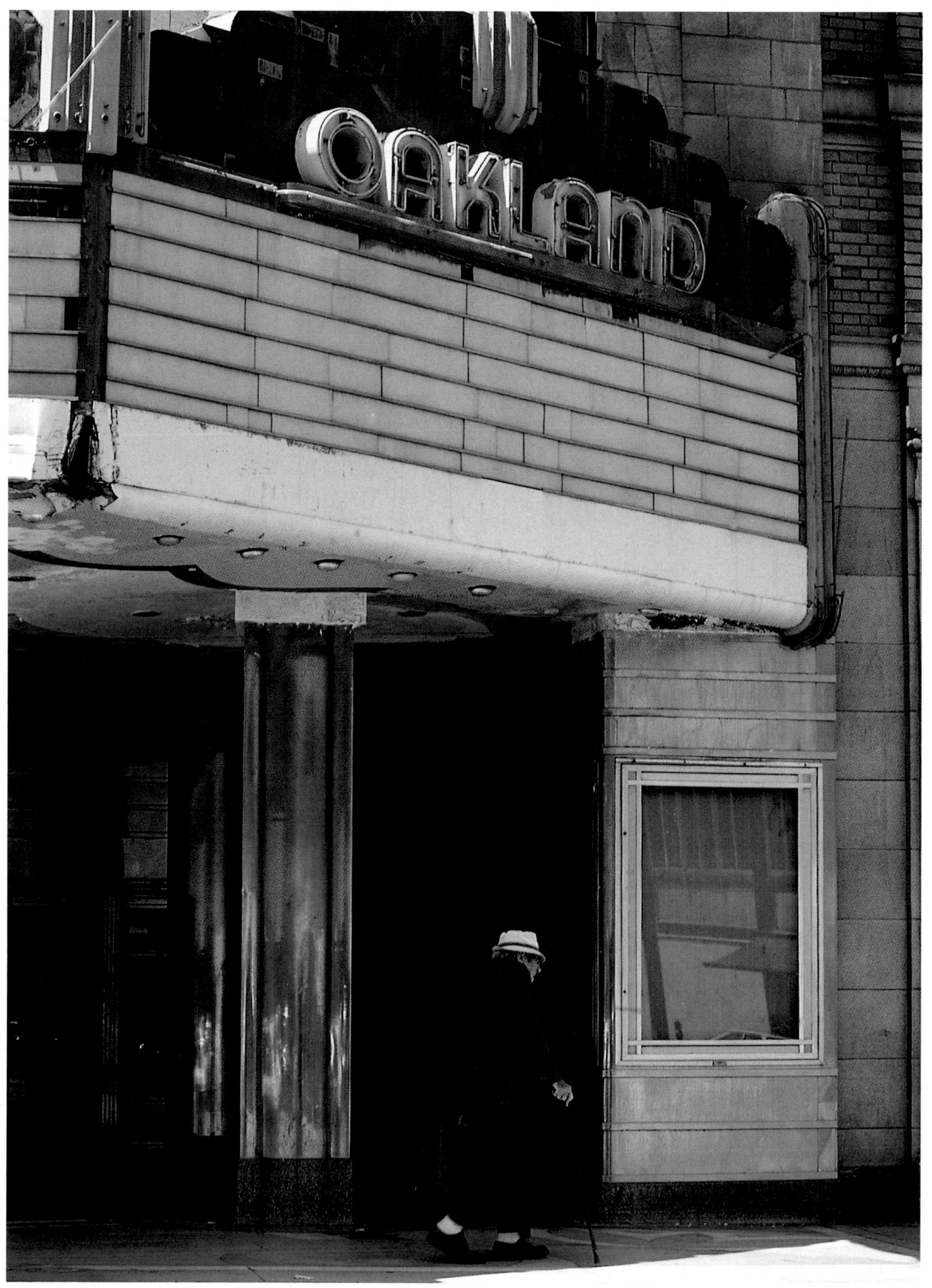

Oakland 18th and Telegraph *June 1982*

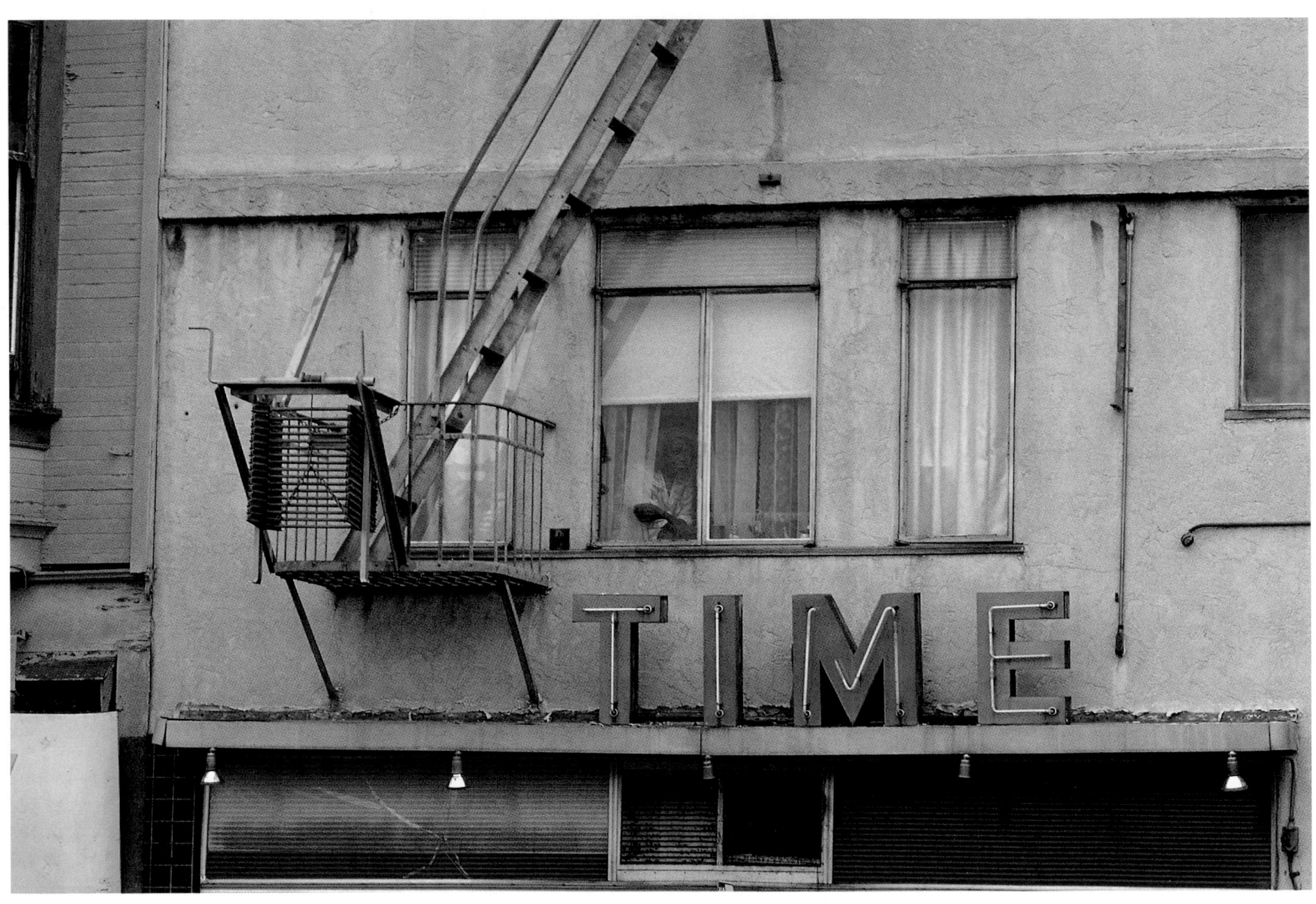

Time   14th near Jefferson   *July 1977*

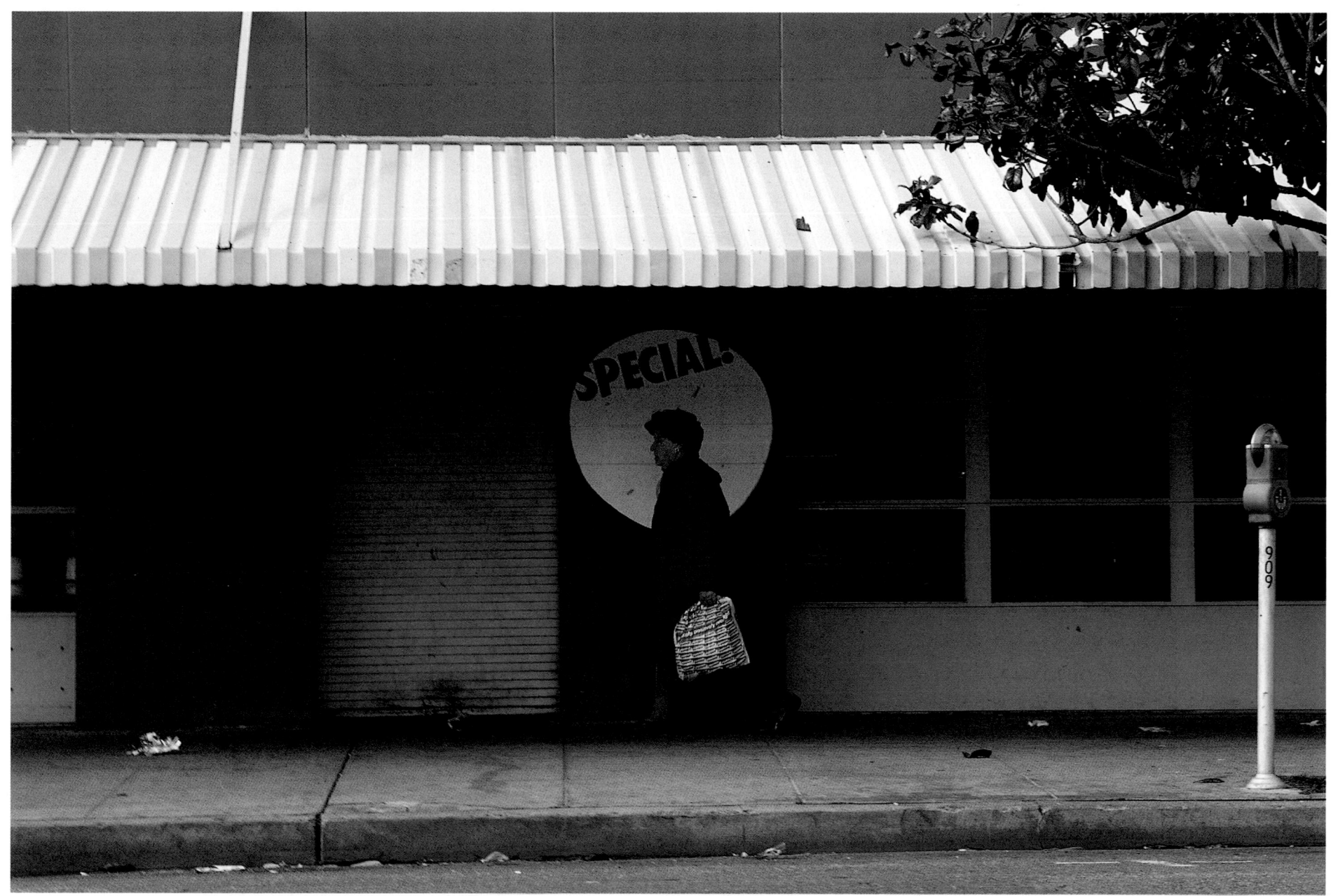

Special Jefferson at 10th *November 1980*

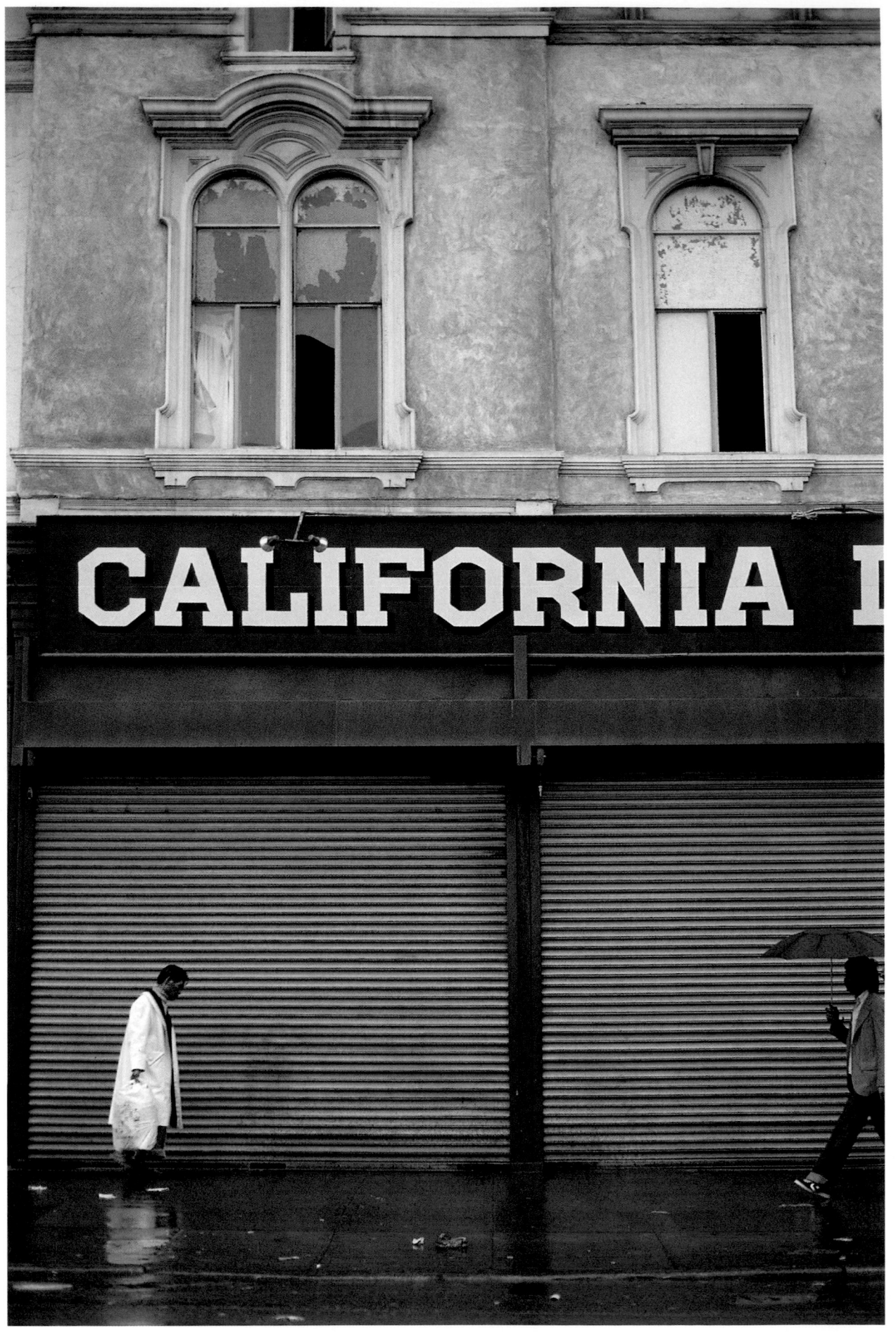

California 9th and Broadway *February 1981*

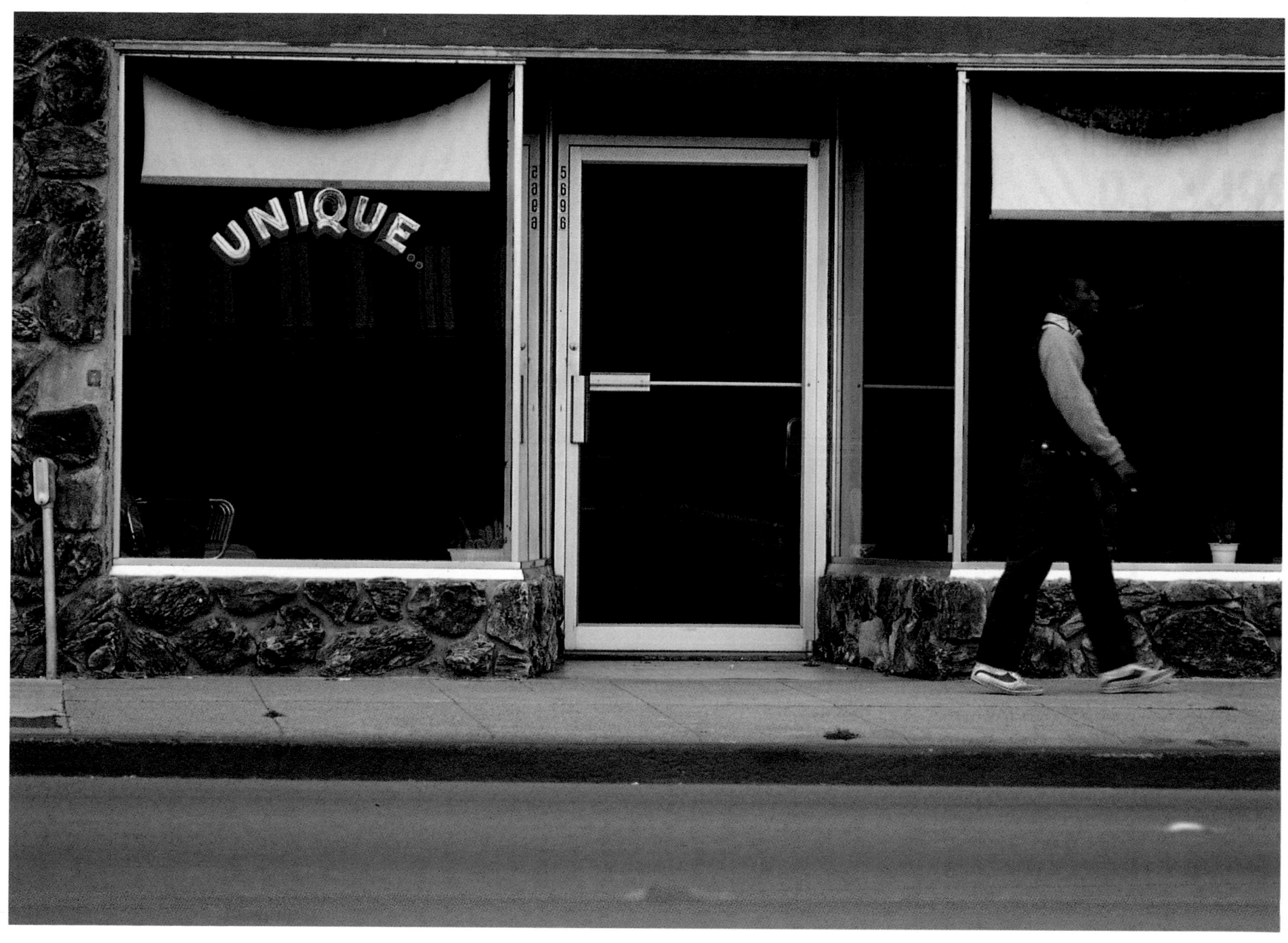

Unique San Pablo Avenue *March 1982*

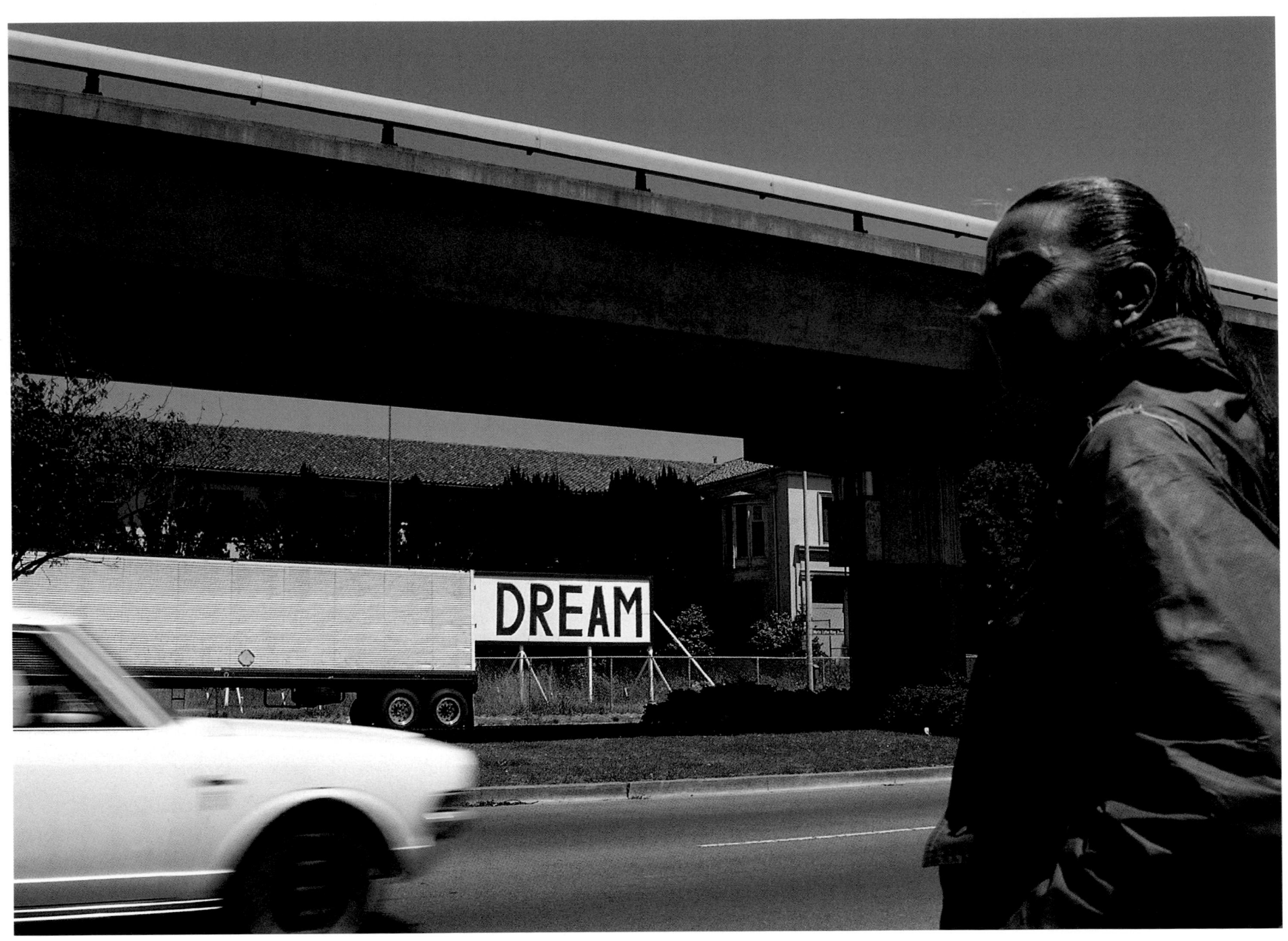

Dream Martin Luther King Jr. Way *June 1986*

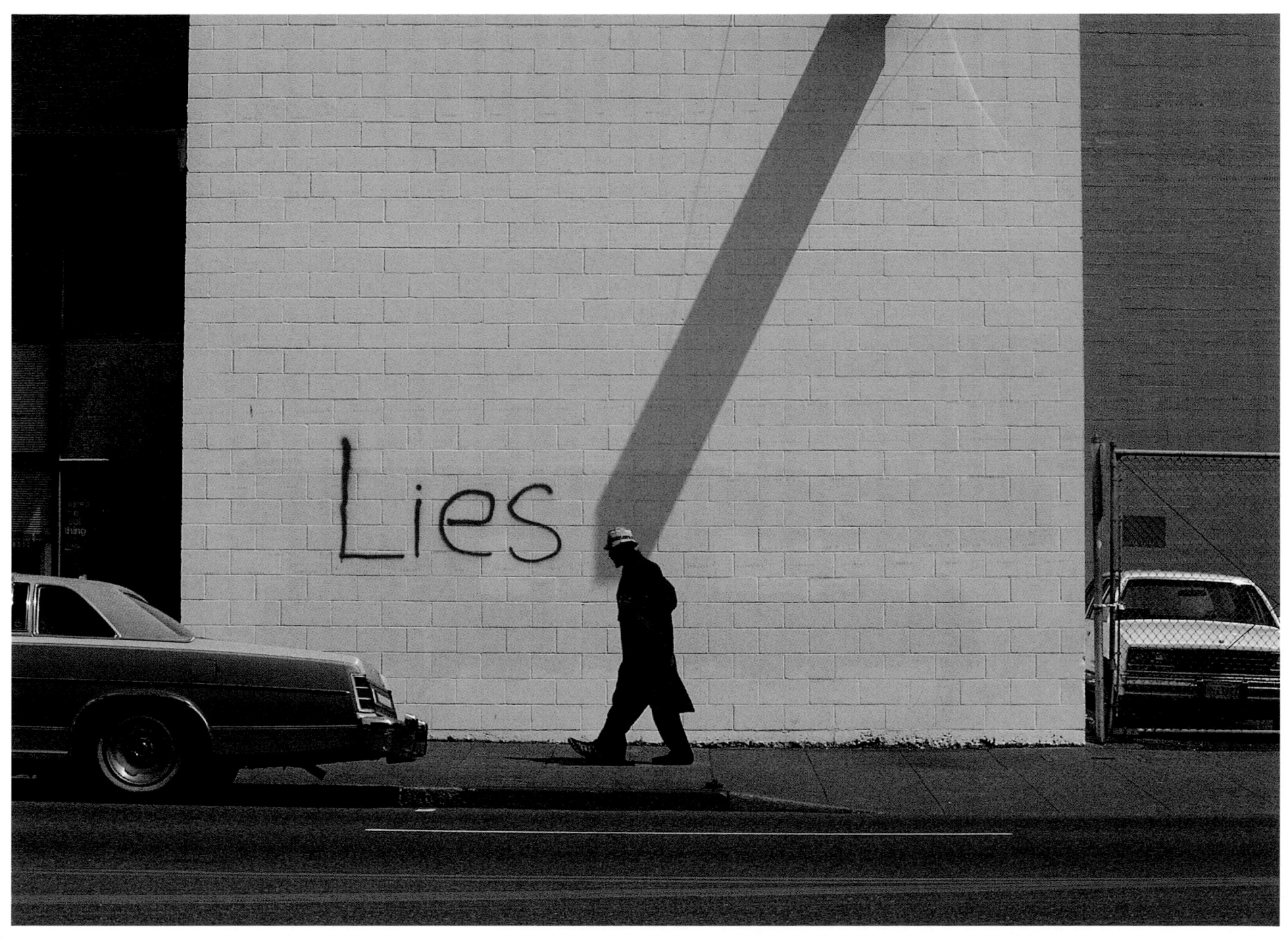

Lies   Telegraph Avenue near 21st   *May 1985*

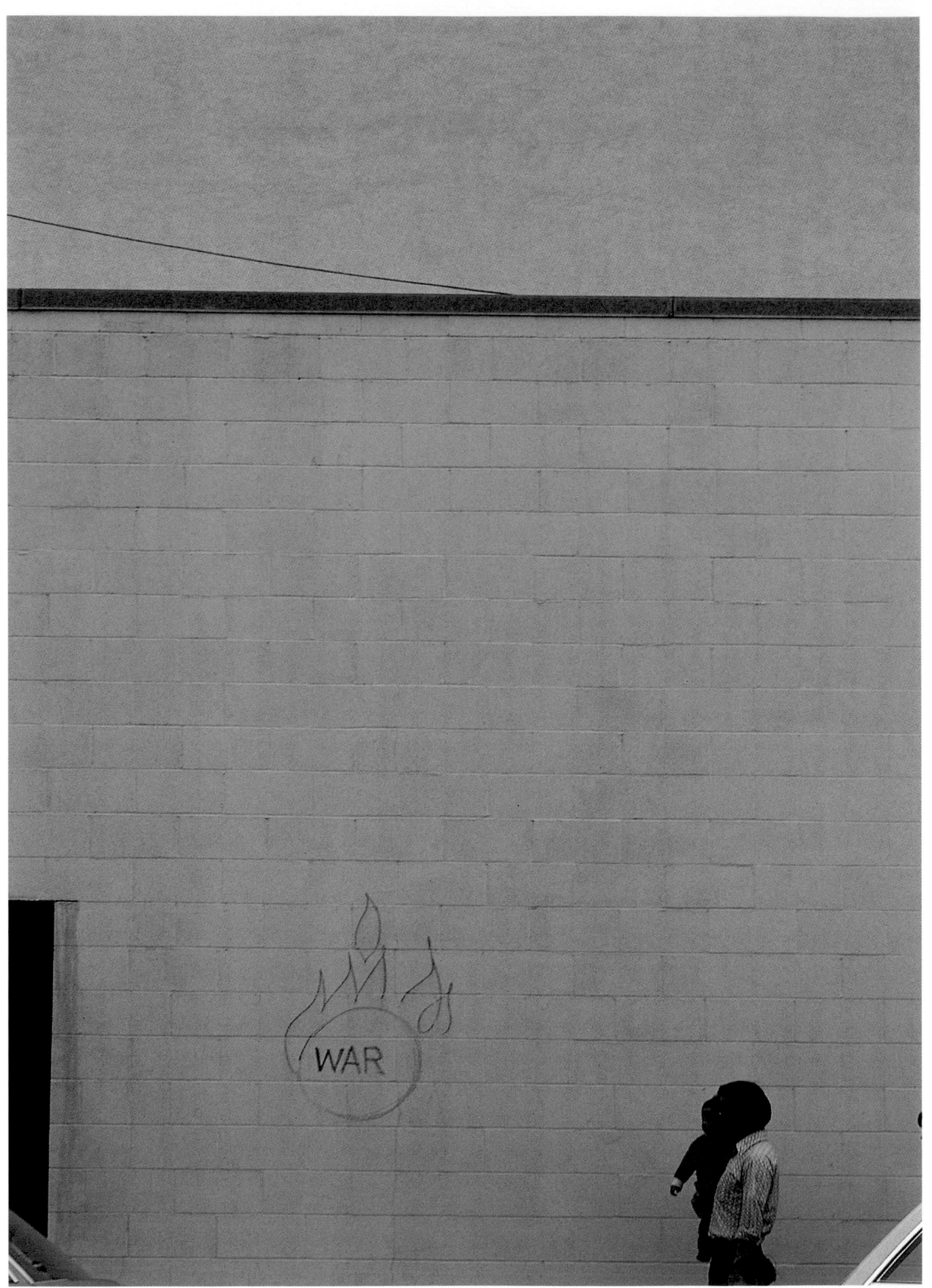

War 8th and Harrison *April 1981*

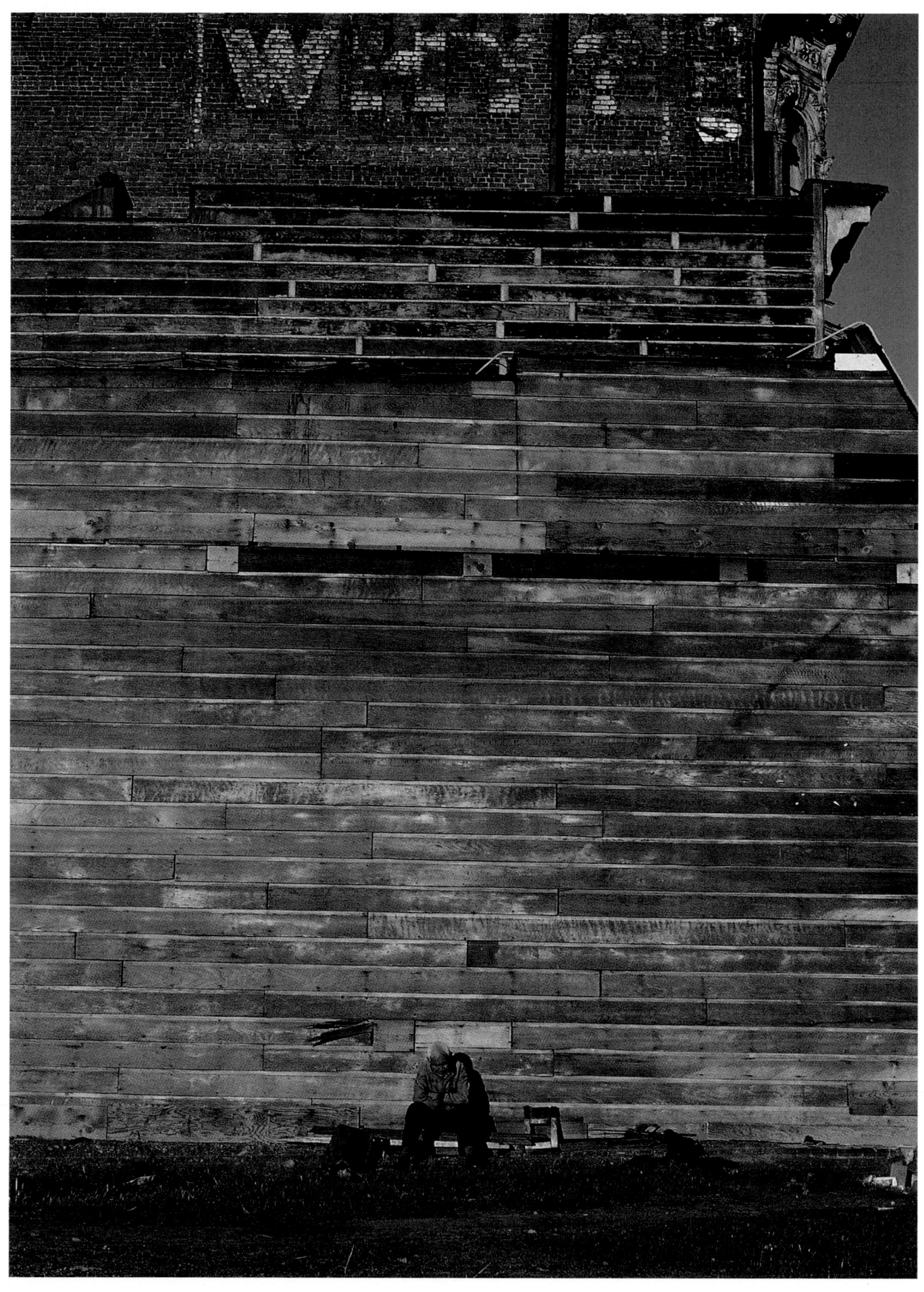

Why 7th and Washington *December 1977*

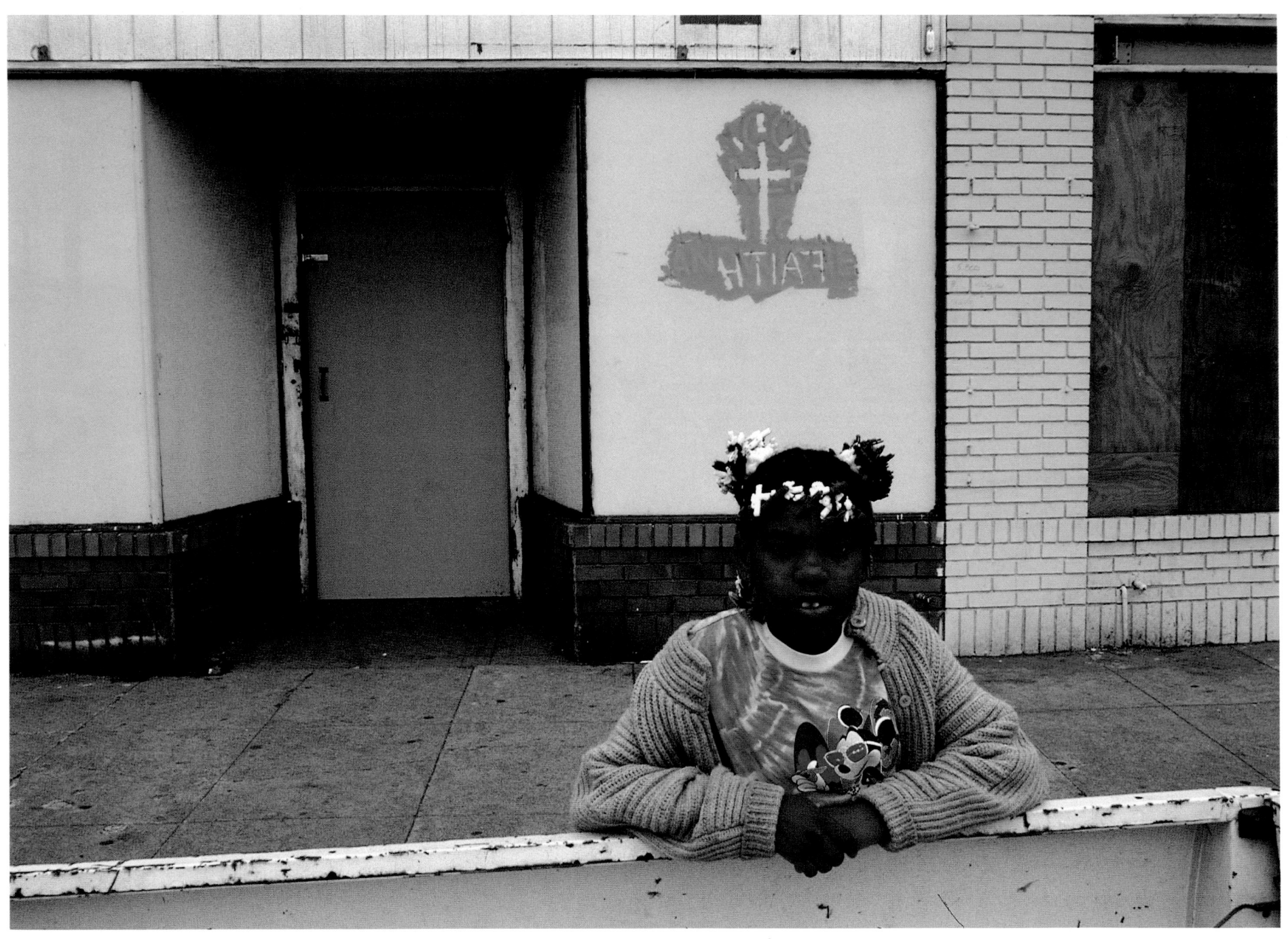

Faith   San Pablo Avenue   *April 1992*

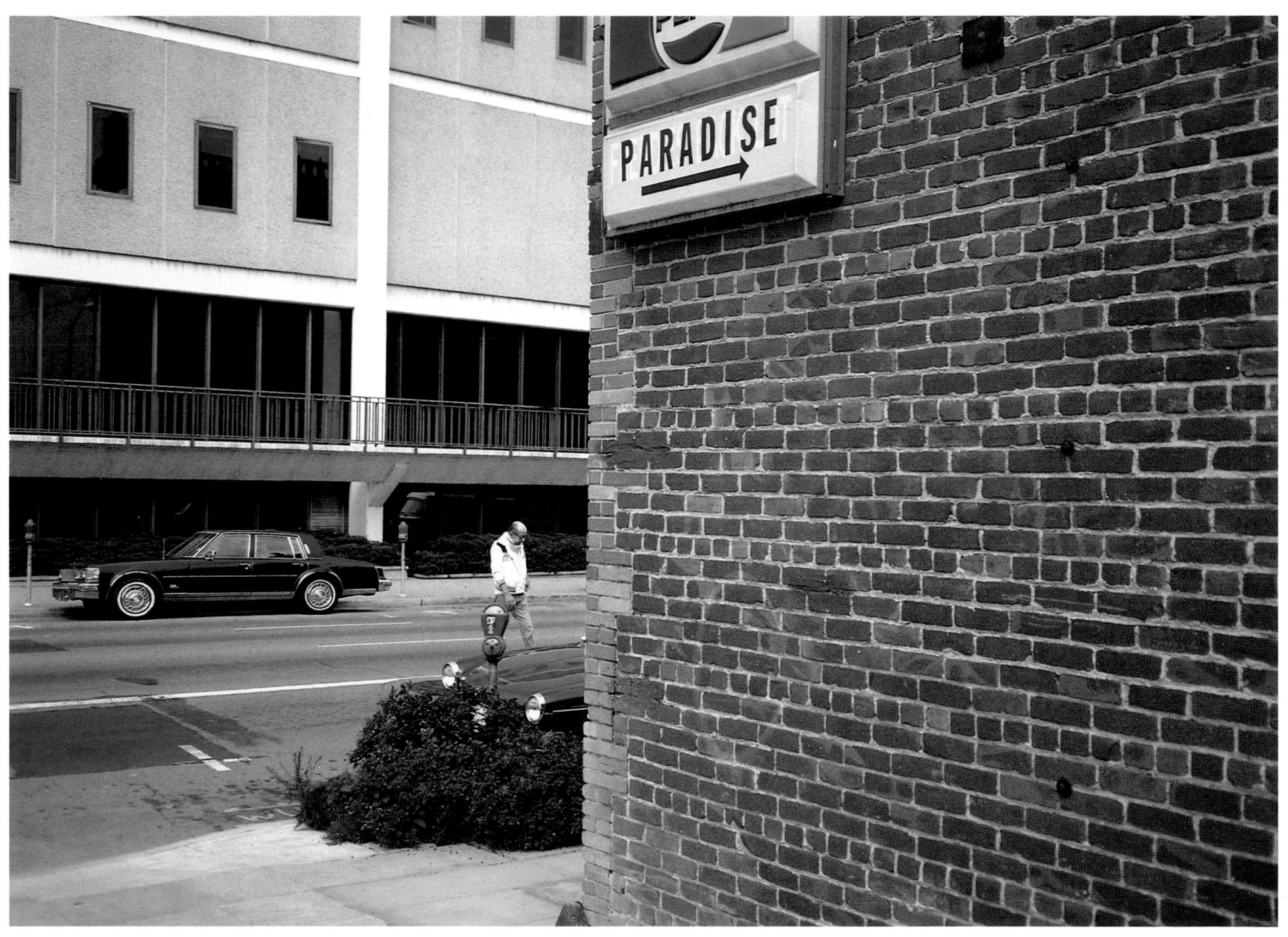

Paradise   12th and Oak   *August 1991*

THE HERE AND NOW

Yet there is hope.

Since I wrote the introduction, a report has been released which points to a 12 percent decline in crime and a 62 percent decline in drive-by shootings.

Two girls dressed in traditional church attire mixed with Kinte cloth look as though they've just been informed of the news. Maybe they, and the two Asian American girls eating ice cream, will escape the scourge of bigotry and racial misinterpretations which have been handed down through each succeeding ignorant generation.

It takes the artist to show that man is capable of throwing off this bondage.

Gospel singers in their blue and white robes standing in the lobby of the beautiful art deco palace, The Paramount, show men and women at their best.

The artist is capable of showing a side of the human experience that the daily tabloids seem incapable of projecting. The artist is capable of refuting all of the sour op-eders and the editorial hand wringing warning against bilingualism and multiculturalism, with one picture. The boy and girl in their lovely Mexican costumes say it all. So does the mural of figures in Bavarian costumes, providing a backdrop for two men engaged in intense conversation. The chorus of many cultures before a Christmas tree. Who would want to extinguish such traditions?

Nagler's pictures have to be read. Read as one reads modern poetry. Every reading revealing a new interpretation.

Surprises.

Riddles.

— *Ishmael Reed*

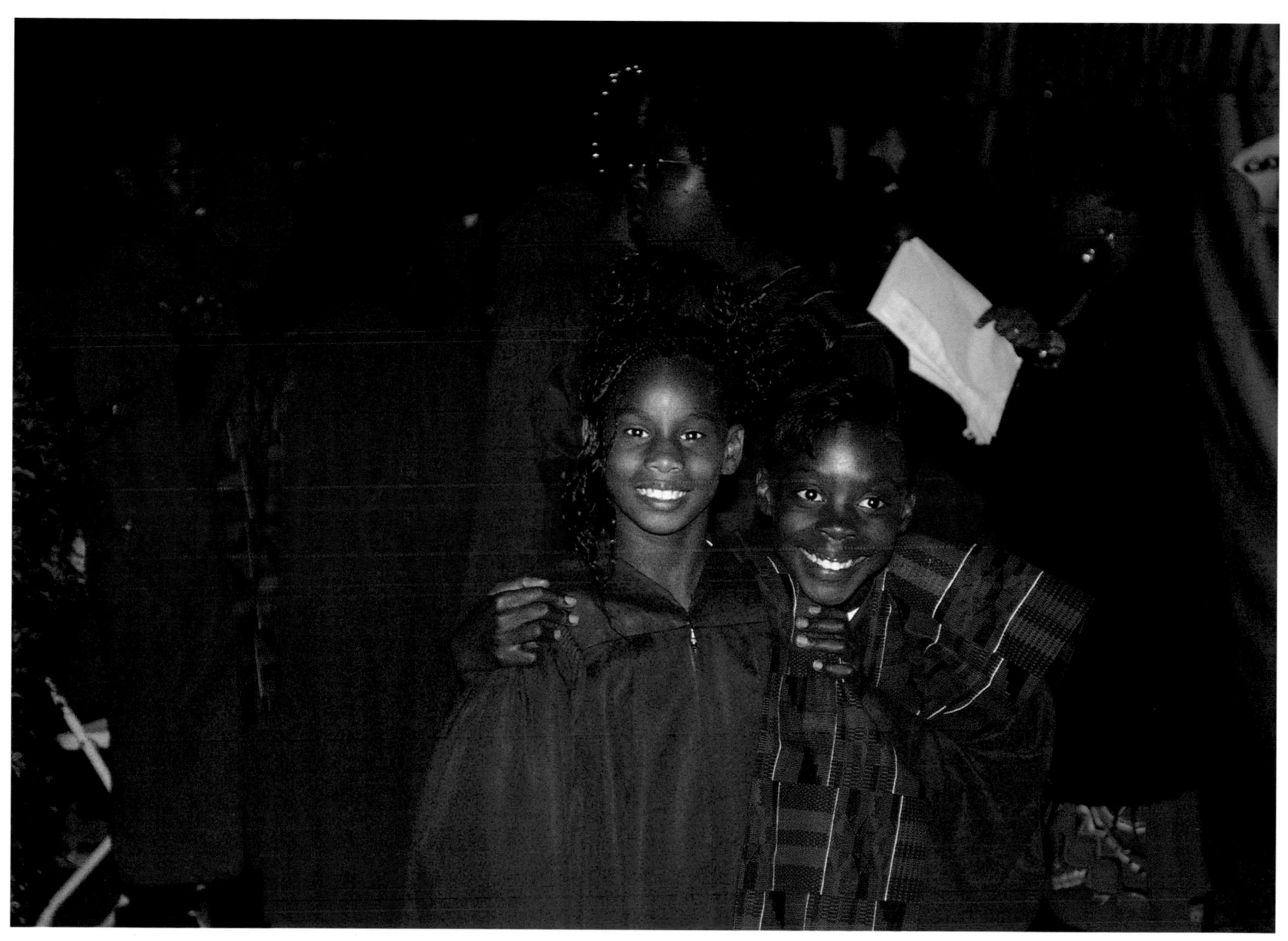

Gospel singers backstage   Oakland Paramount, 21st and Broadway   *September 1992*

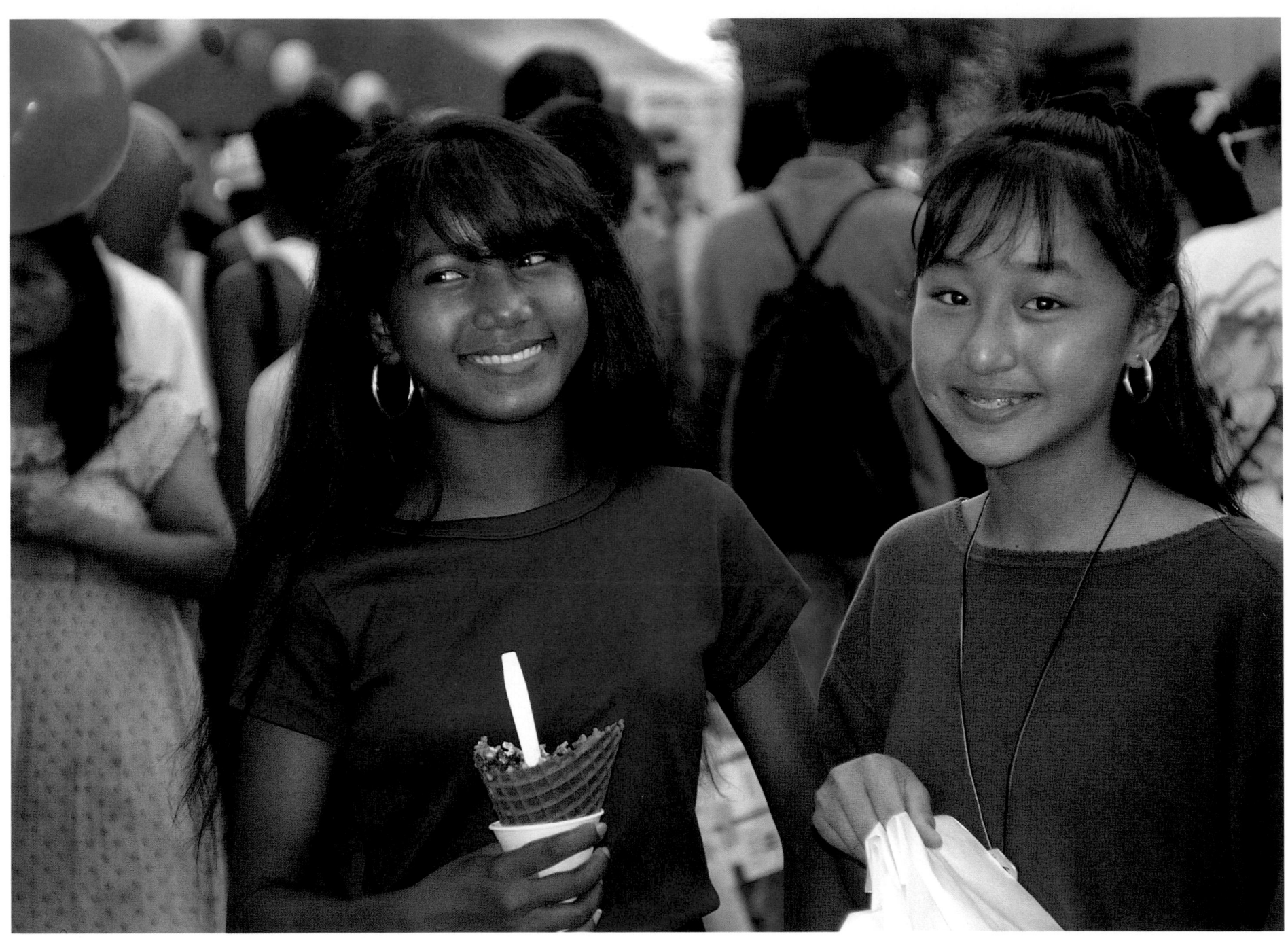

Chinatown Street Fair   *October 1992*

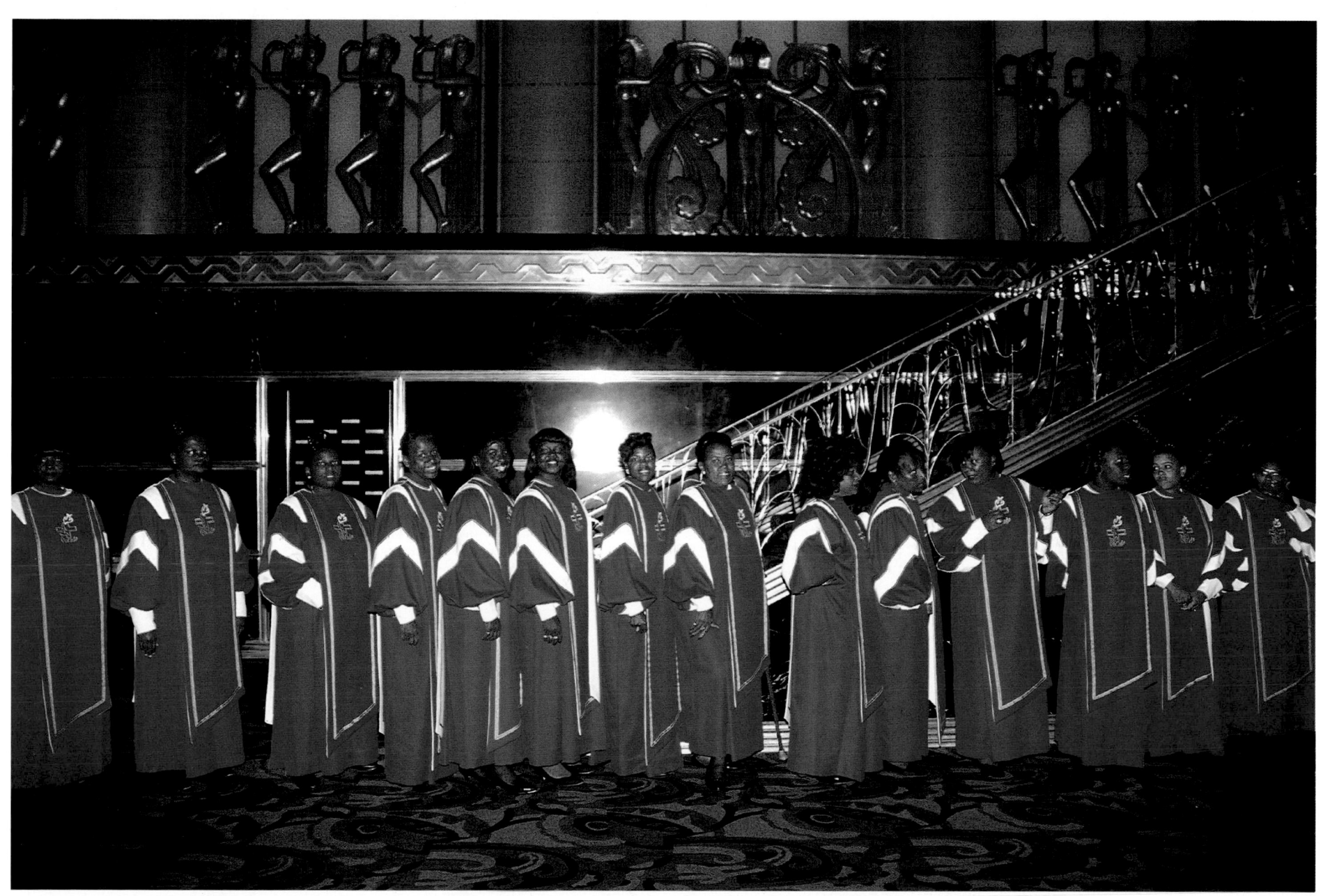

Gospel singers in the lobby   Oakland Paramount, 21st and Broadway   *September 1992*

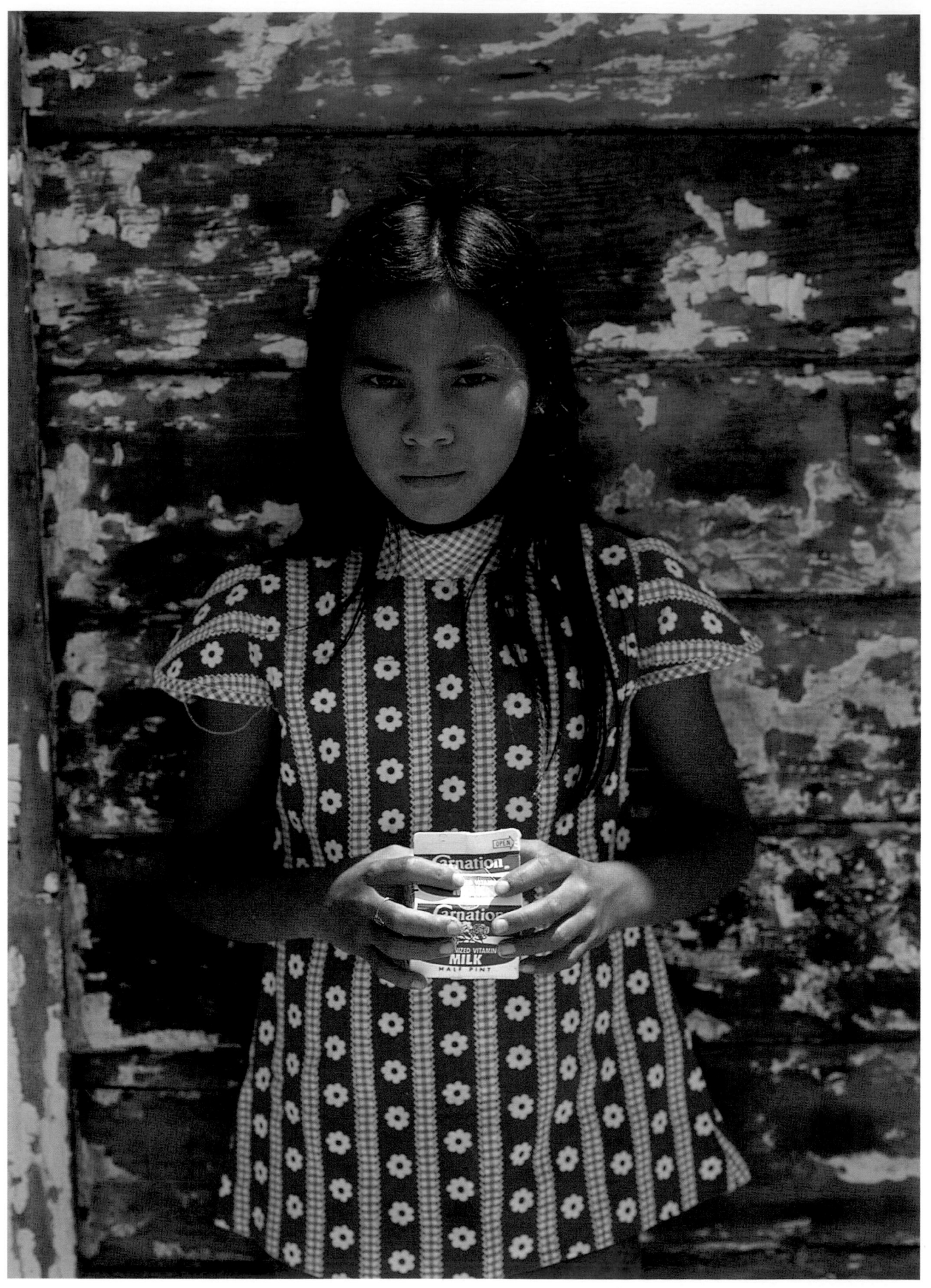

Girl on the street   9th near Martin Luther King Jr. Way   *July 1985*

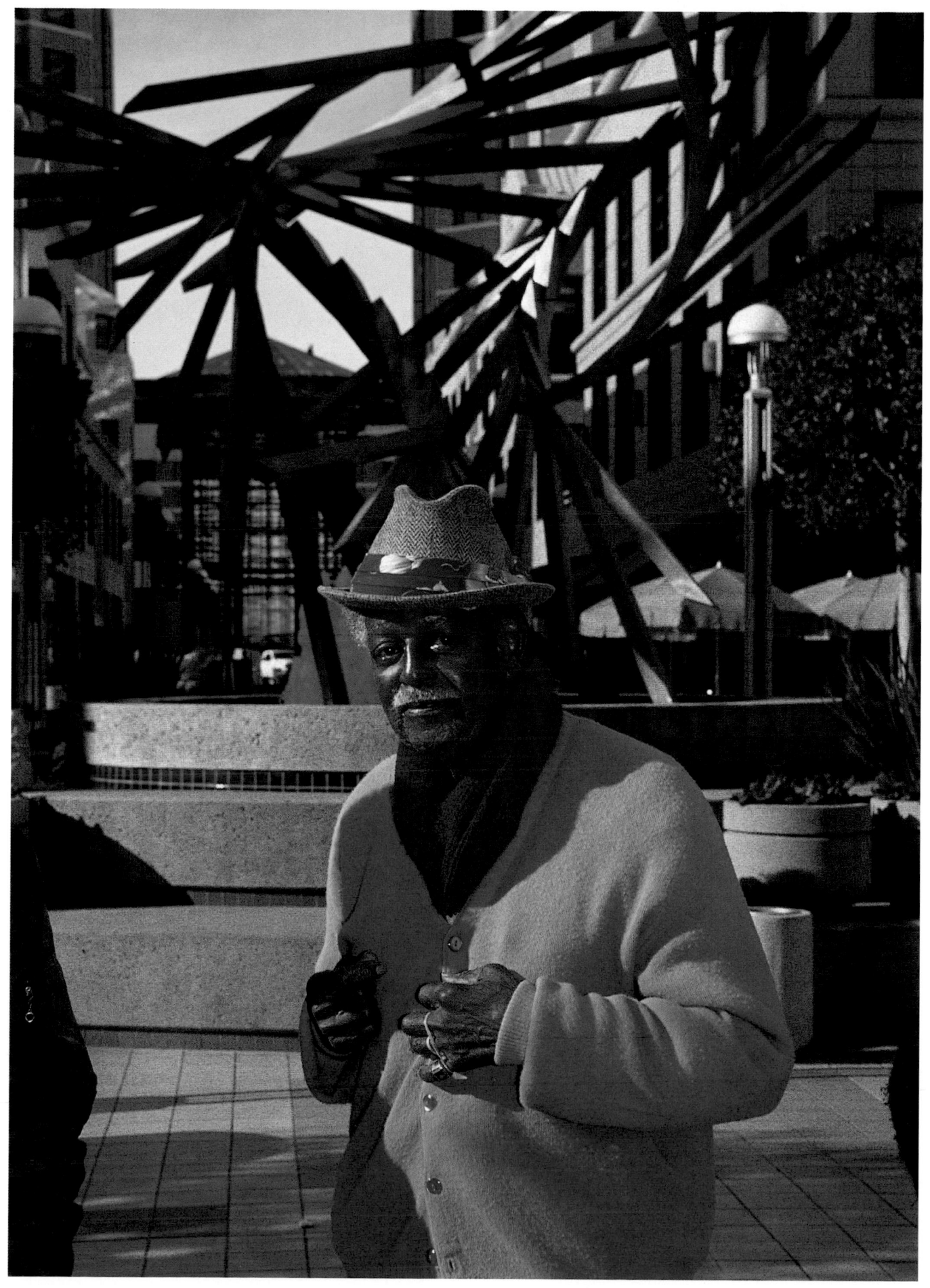

Man and sculpture   City Center Plaza   *December 1992*

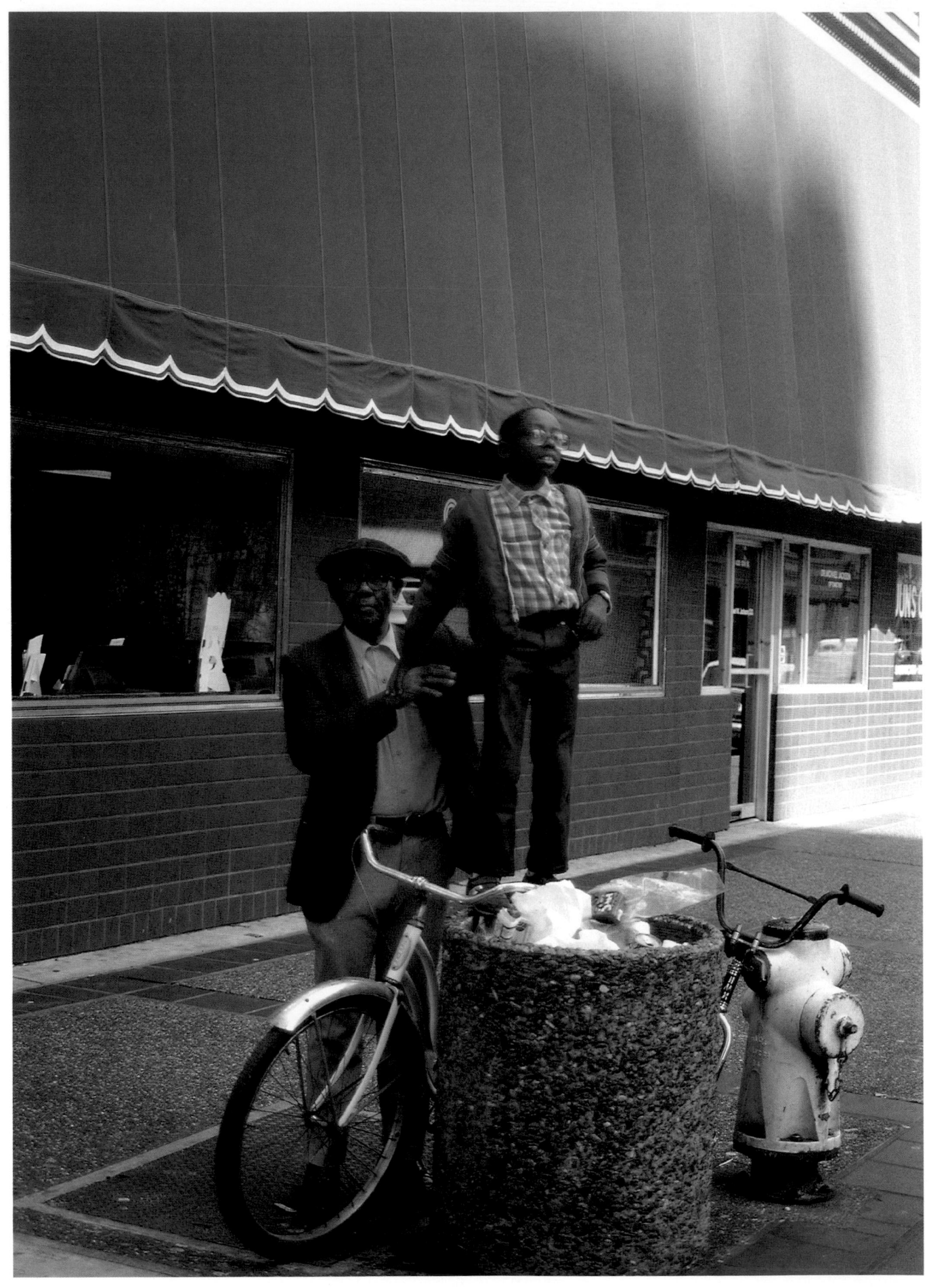

Watching a parade   Broadway at 12th   *March 1984*

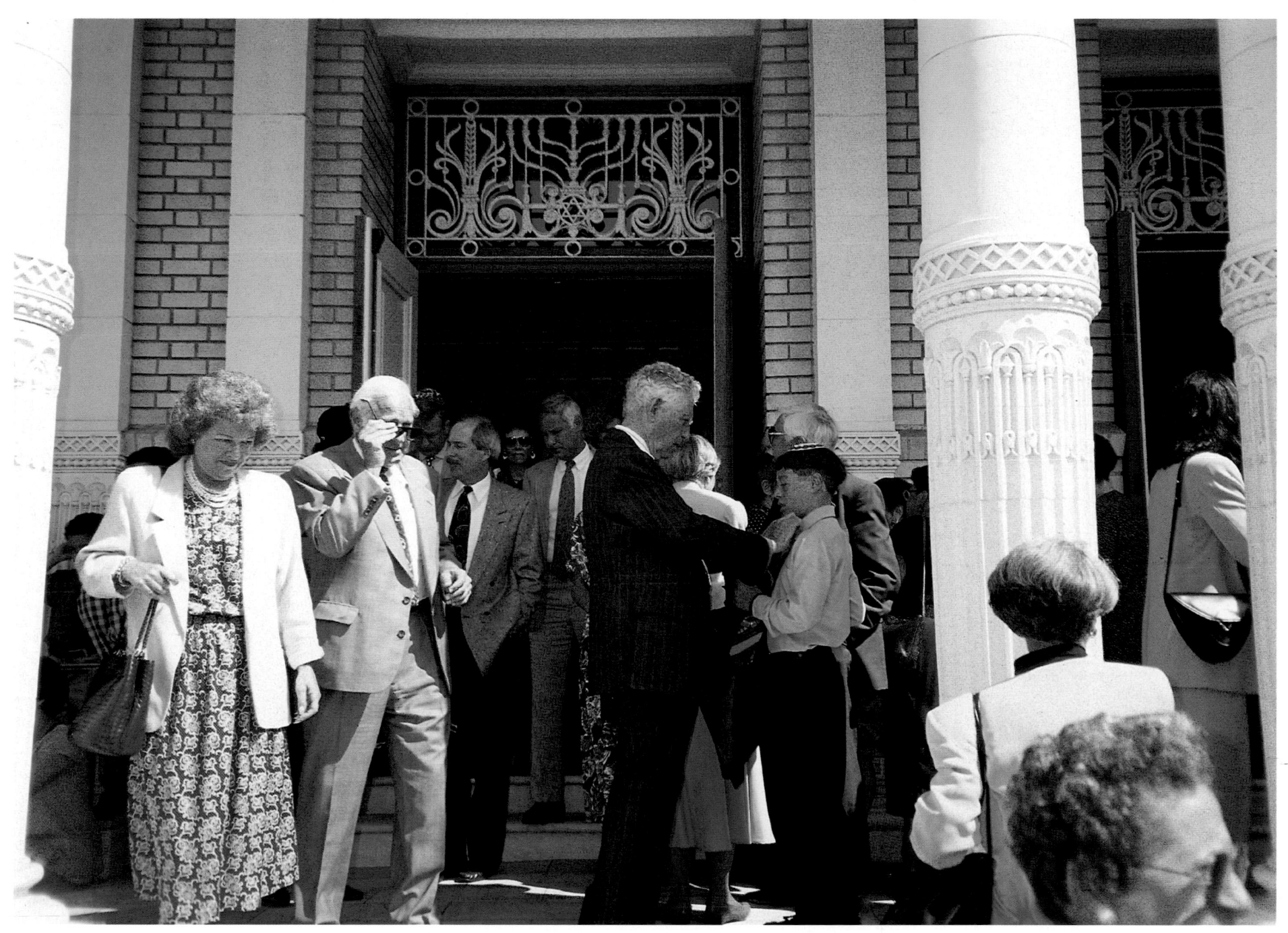

After Rosh Hashanah services   Temple Sinai, 28th near Broadway   *September 1994*

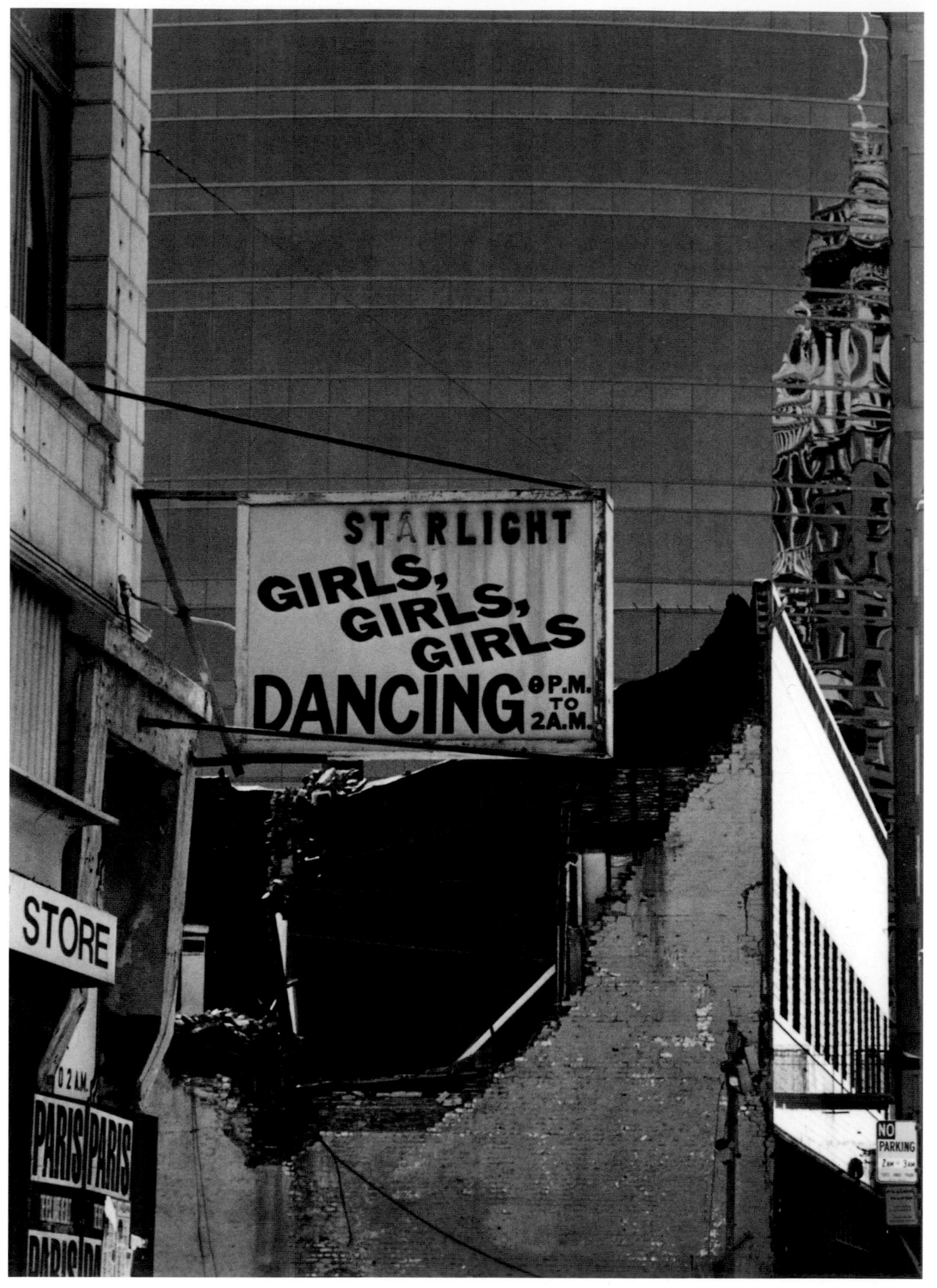

Earthquake Damage   12th and Franklin   *June 1992*

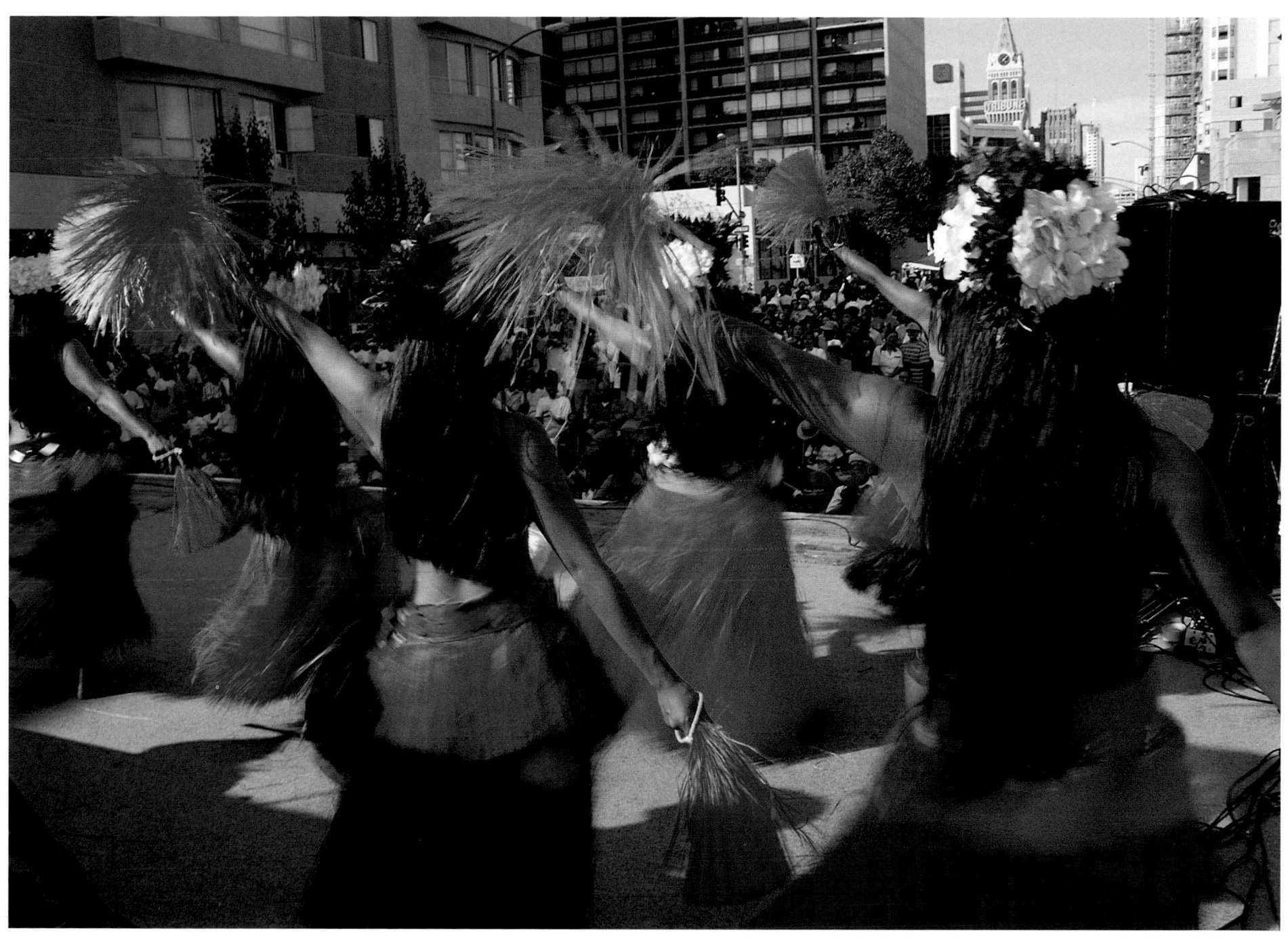

Dancers Chinatown Street Fair *September 1992*

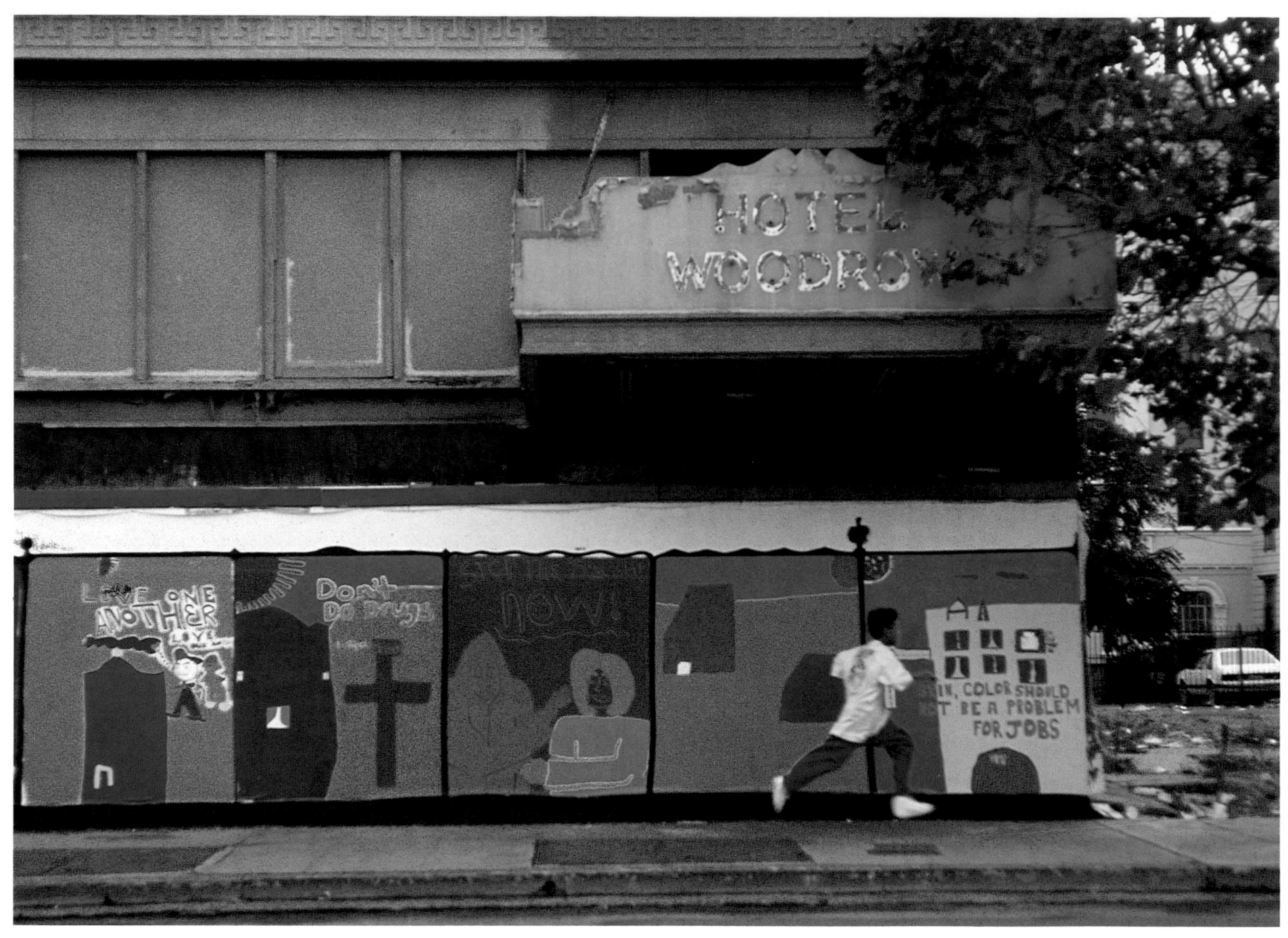

Boy running   14th and Martin Luther King Jr. Way   *October 1993*

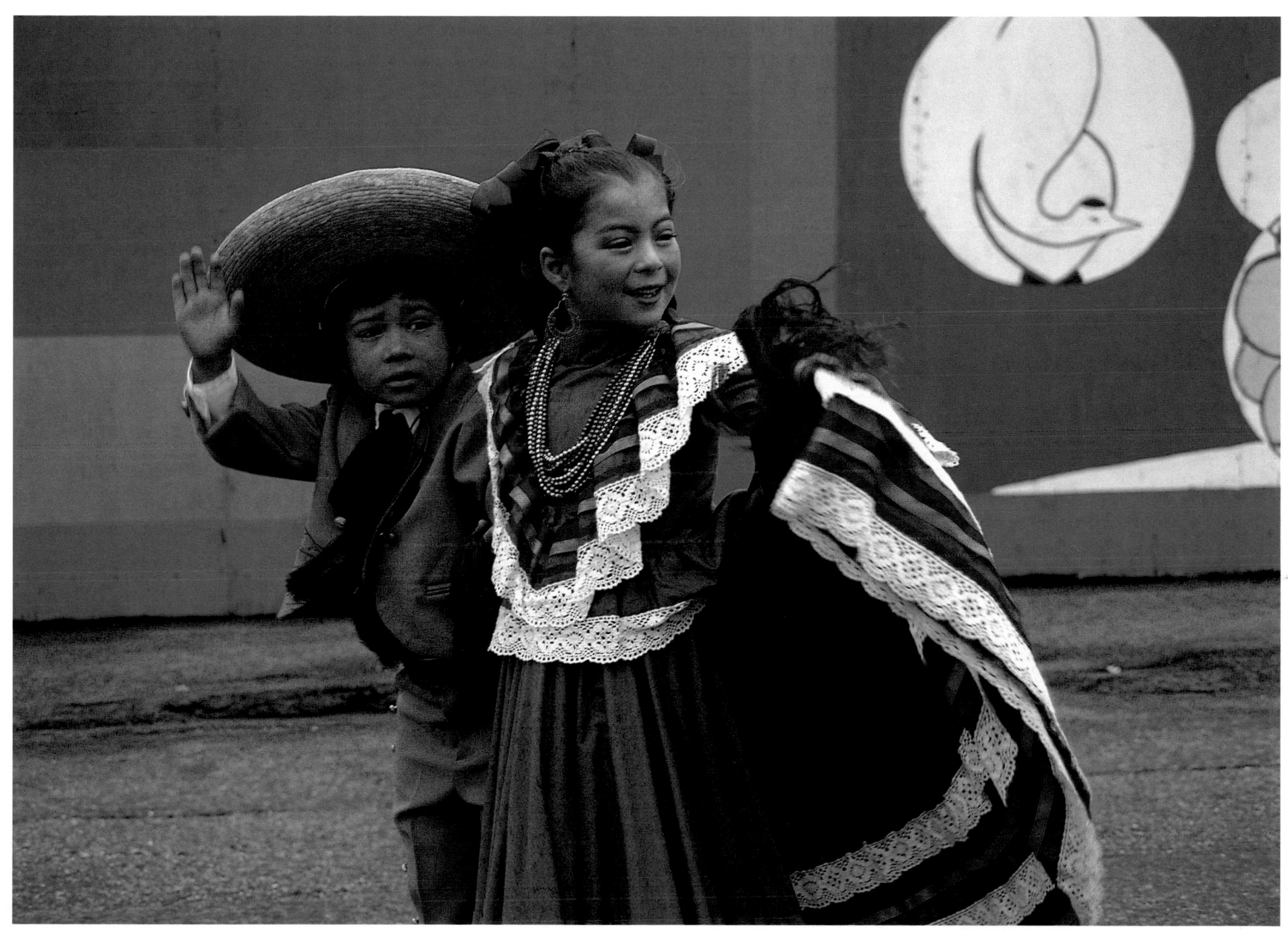

Parade 11th and Broadway *November 1982*

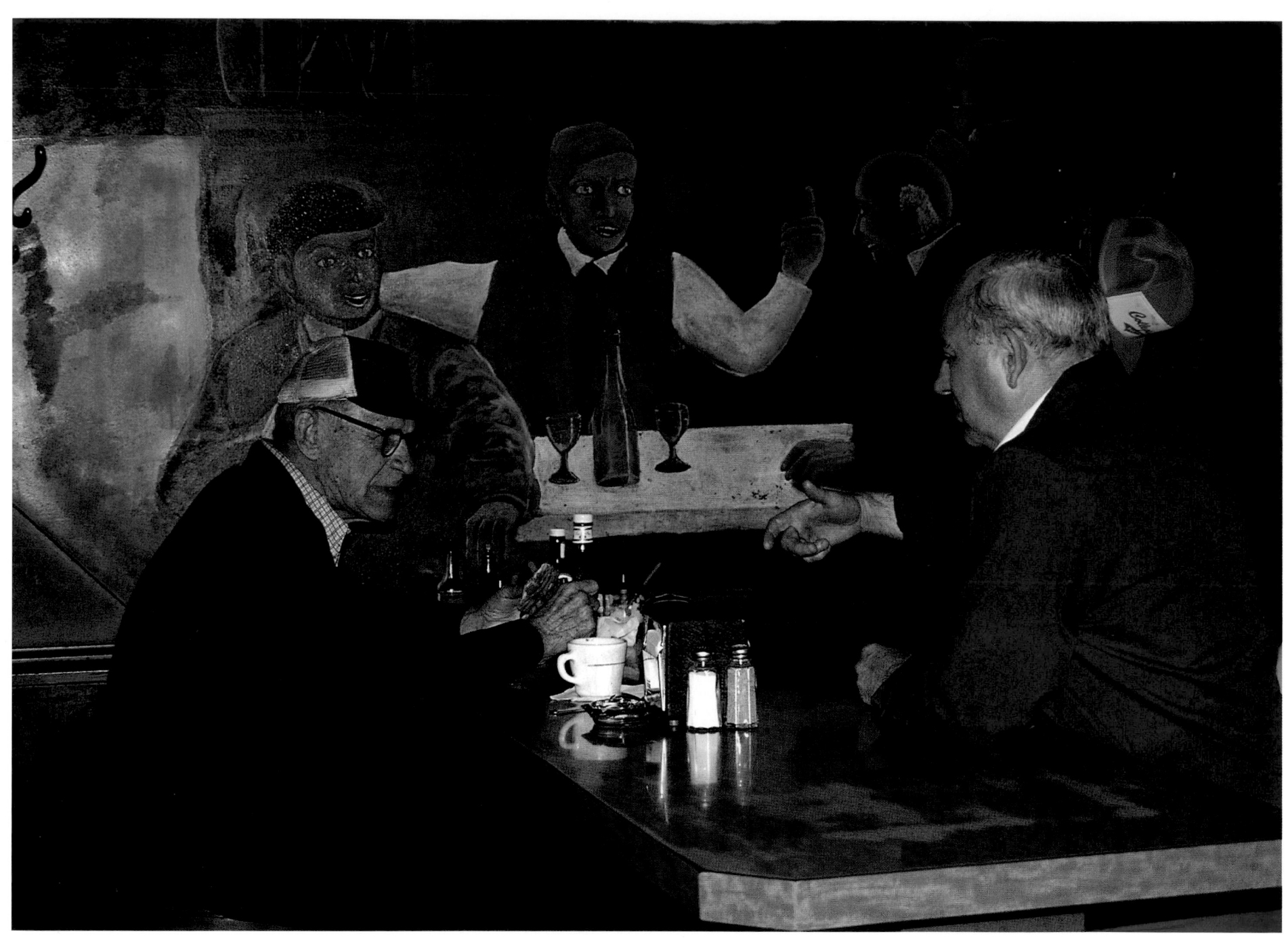

Conversations   Downtown Hofbrau, Broadway at W. Grand Avenue   *May 1983*

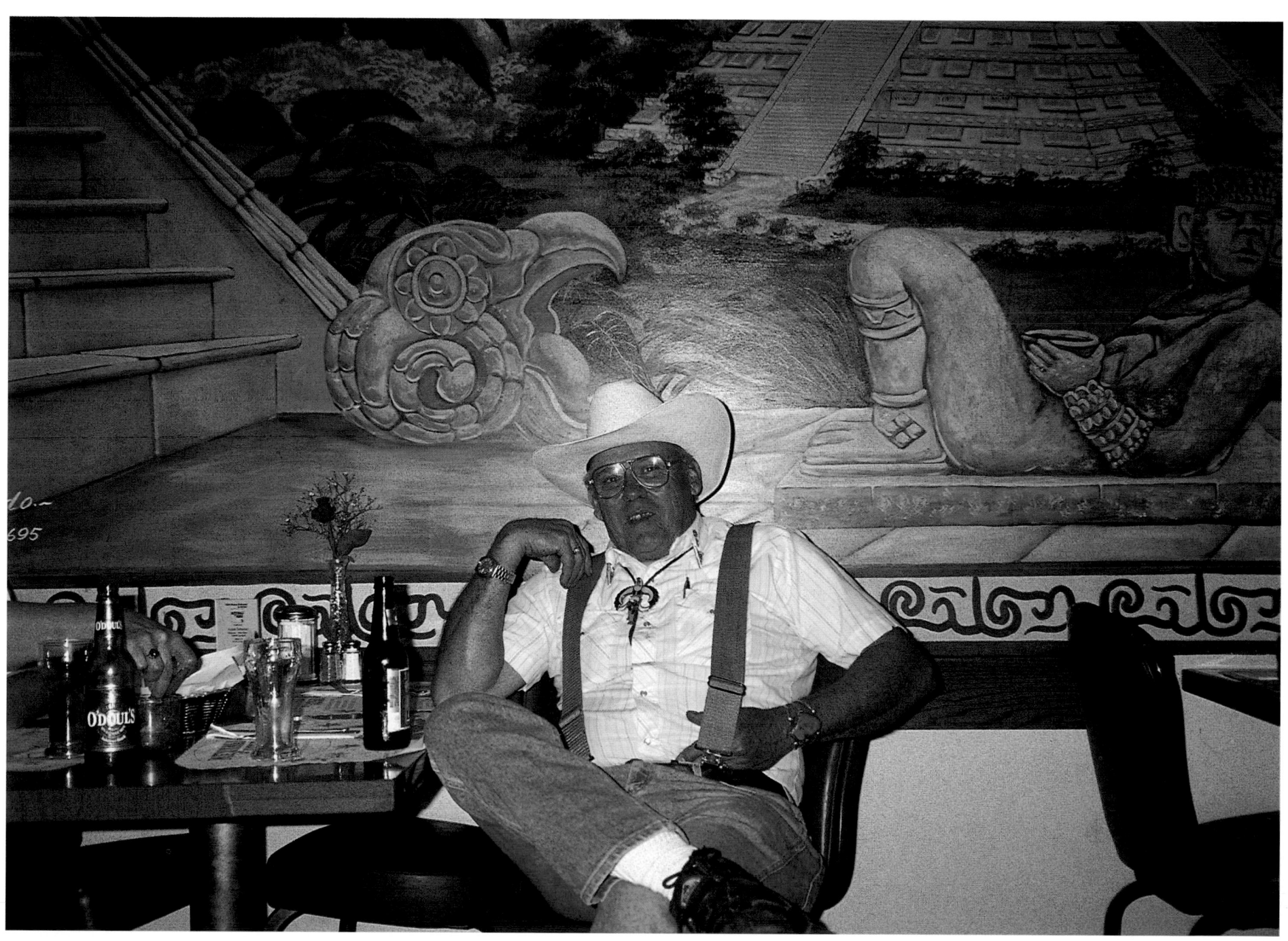

Mexicali Rose restaurant 7th and Clay *September 1993*

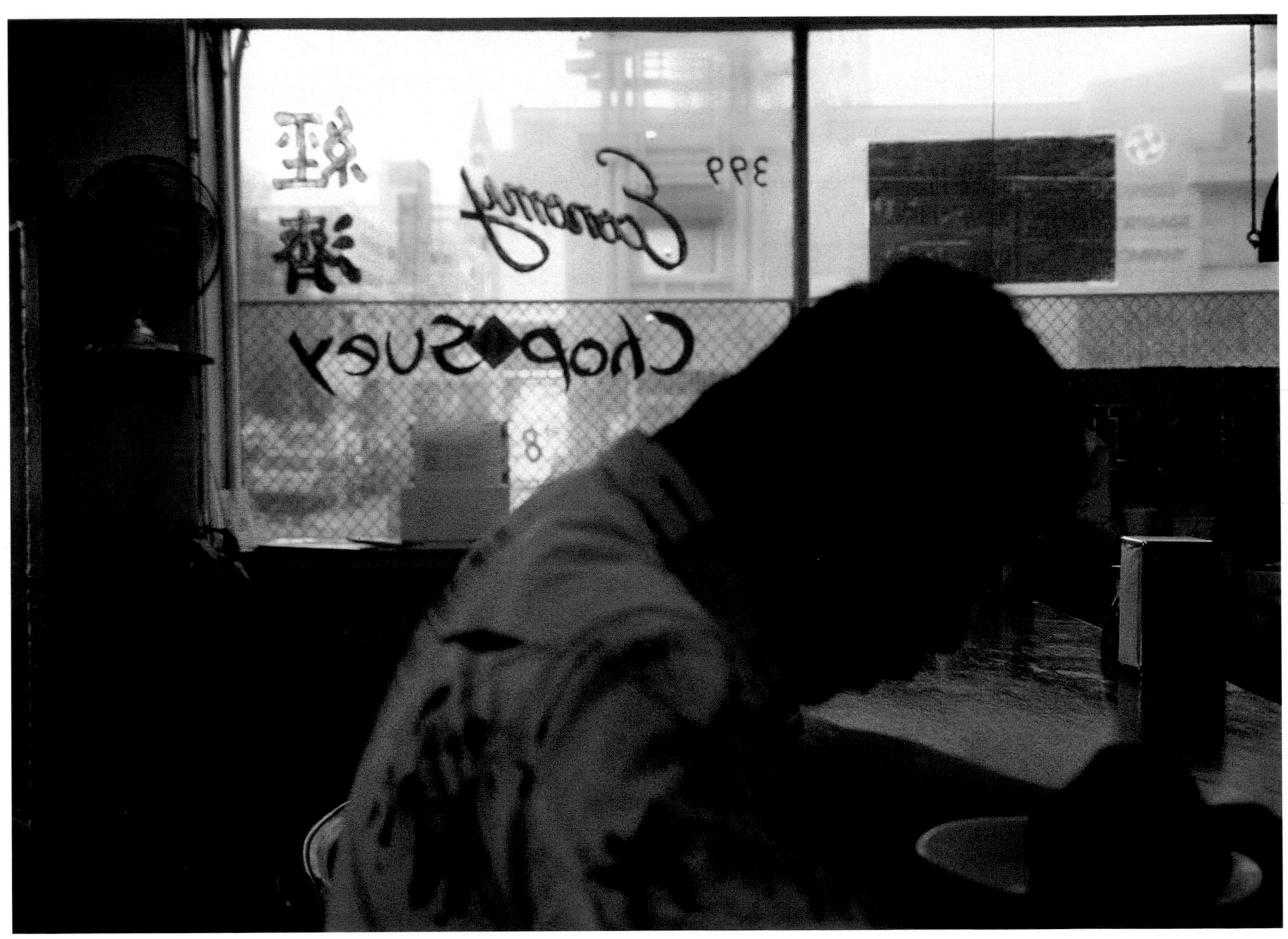

Economy Chop Suey   8th and Franklin   *August 1993*

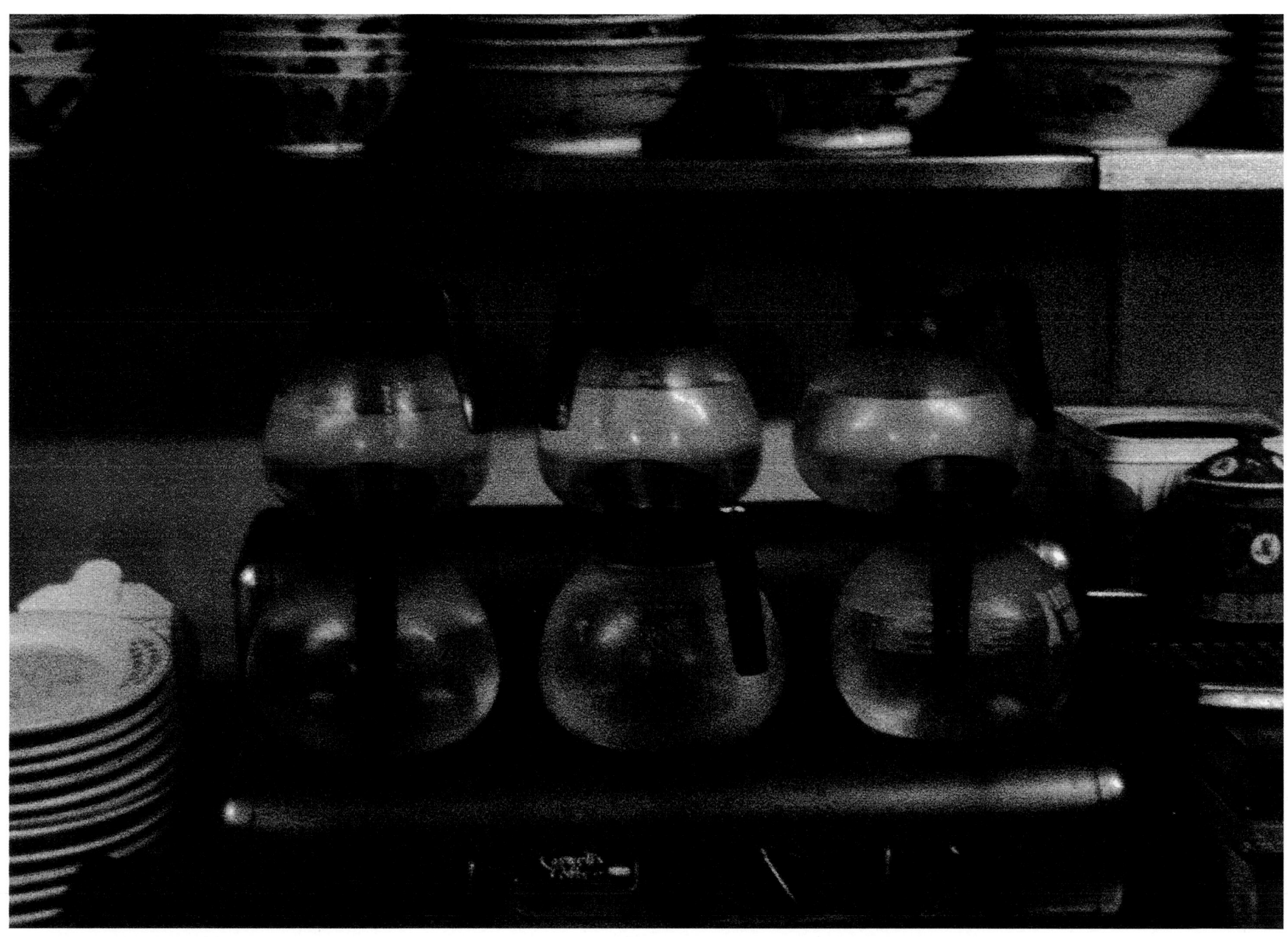

Restaurant interior Chinatown *November 1991*

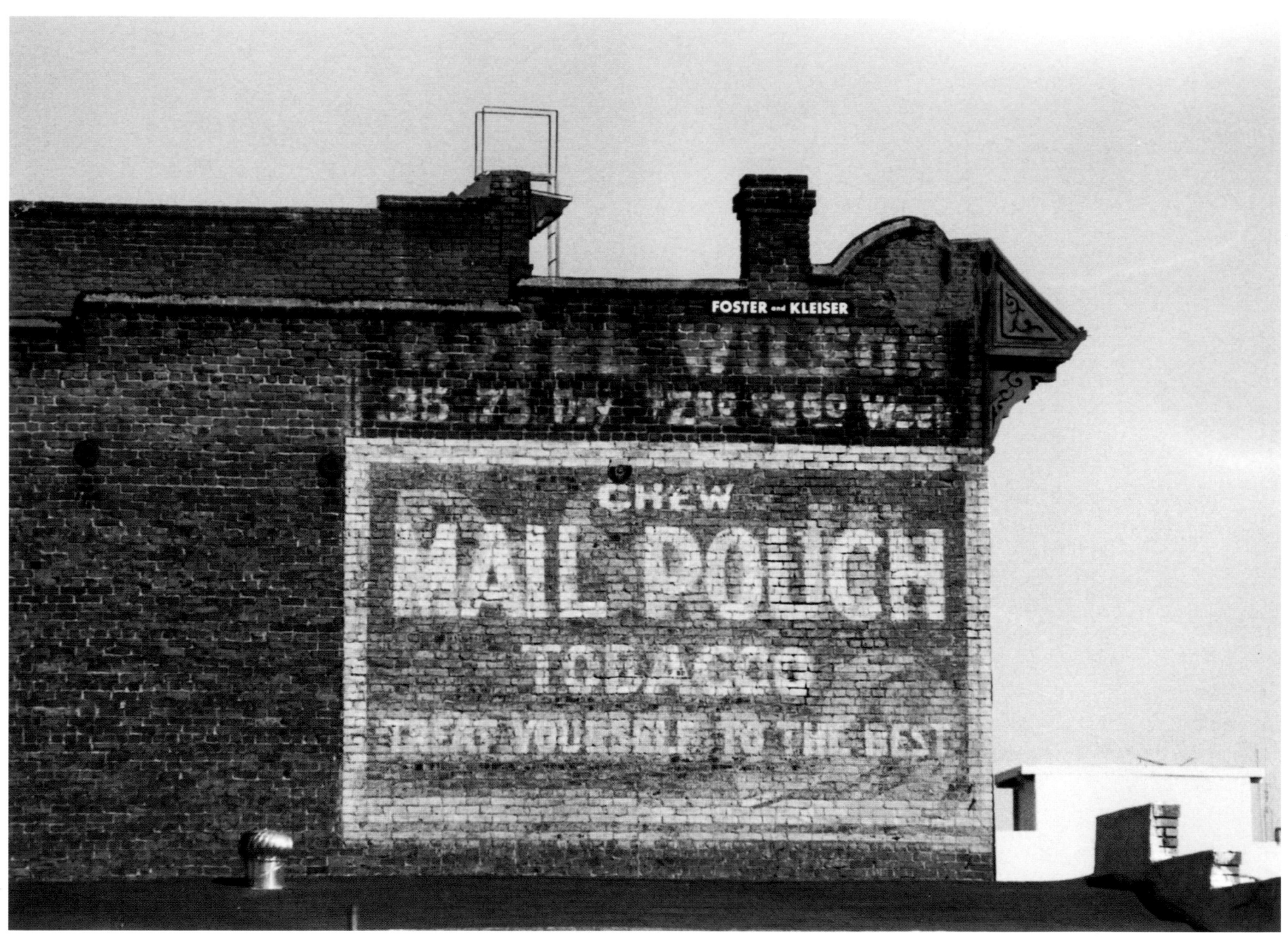

Mail Pouch Tobacco   7th and Broadway   *July 1992*

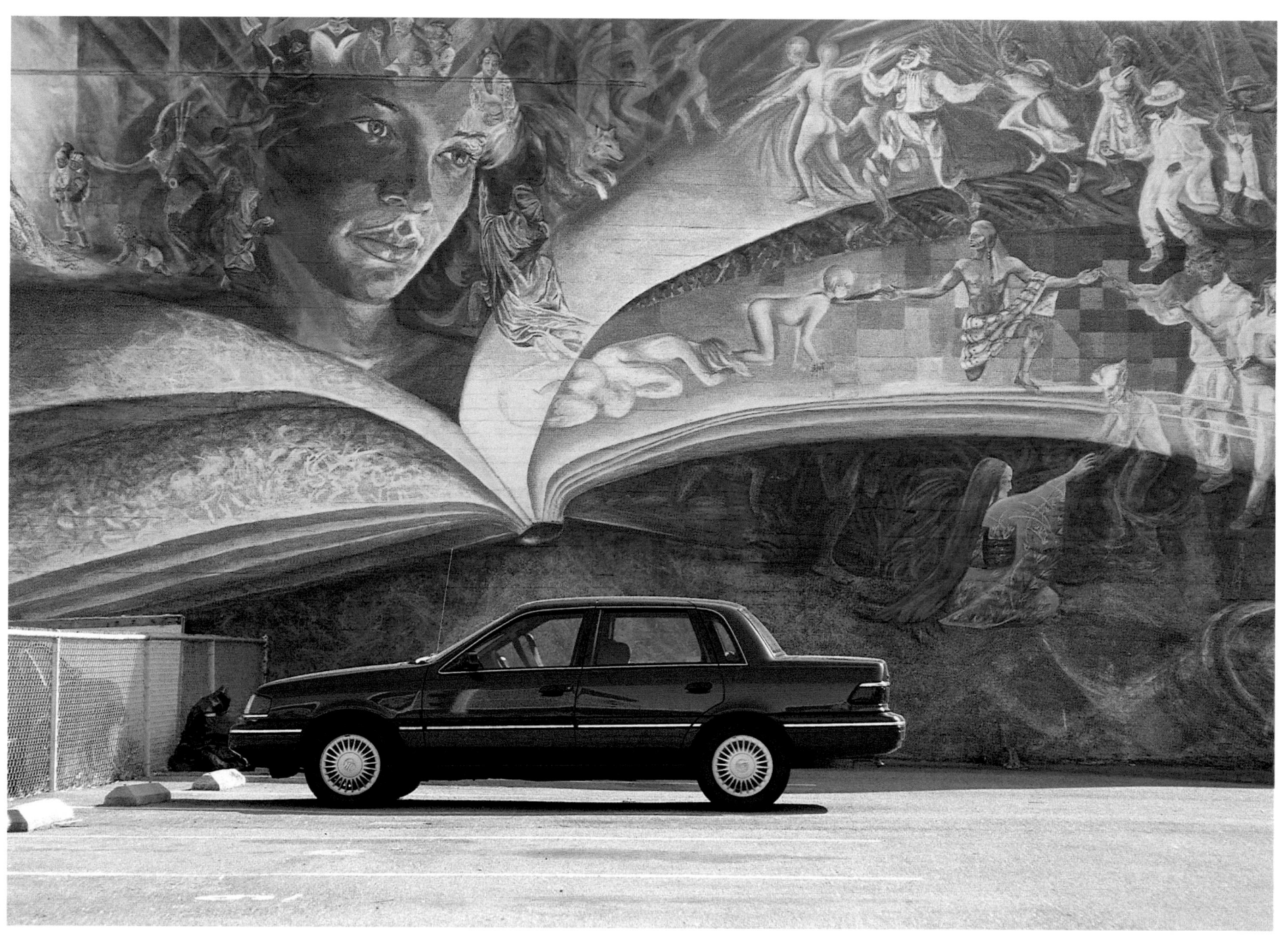

Mural   12th and Oak   *August 1992*

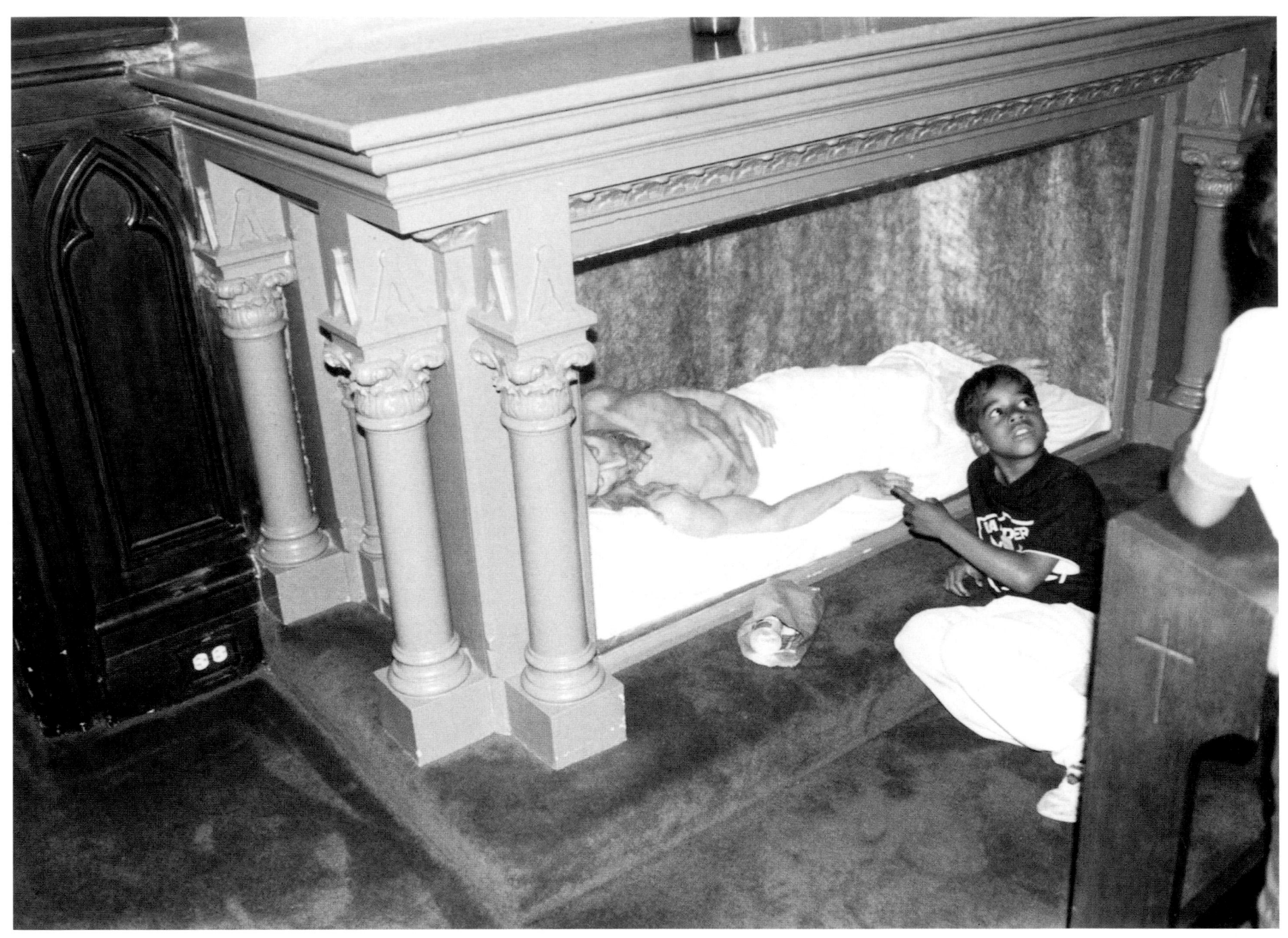

Old Saint Mary's Church   8th and Jefferson   *May 1992*

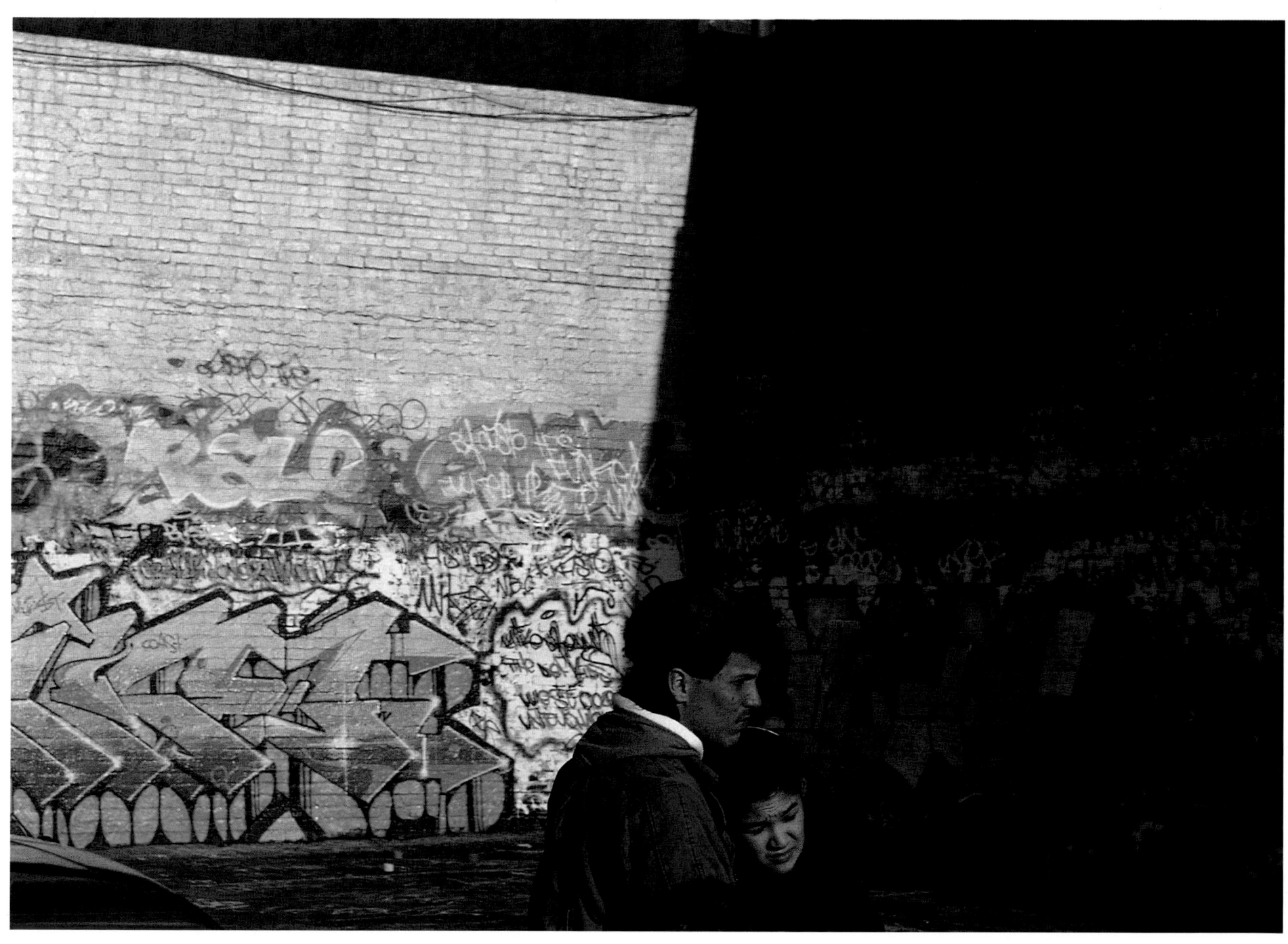

Graffiti hug   17th near Martin Luther King Jr. Way   *June 1987*

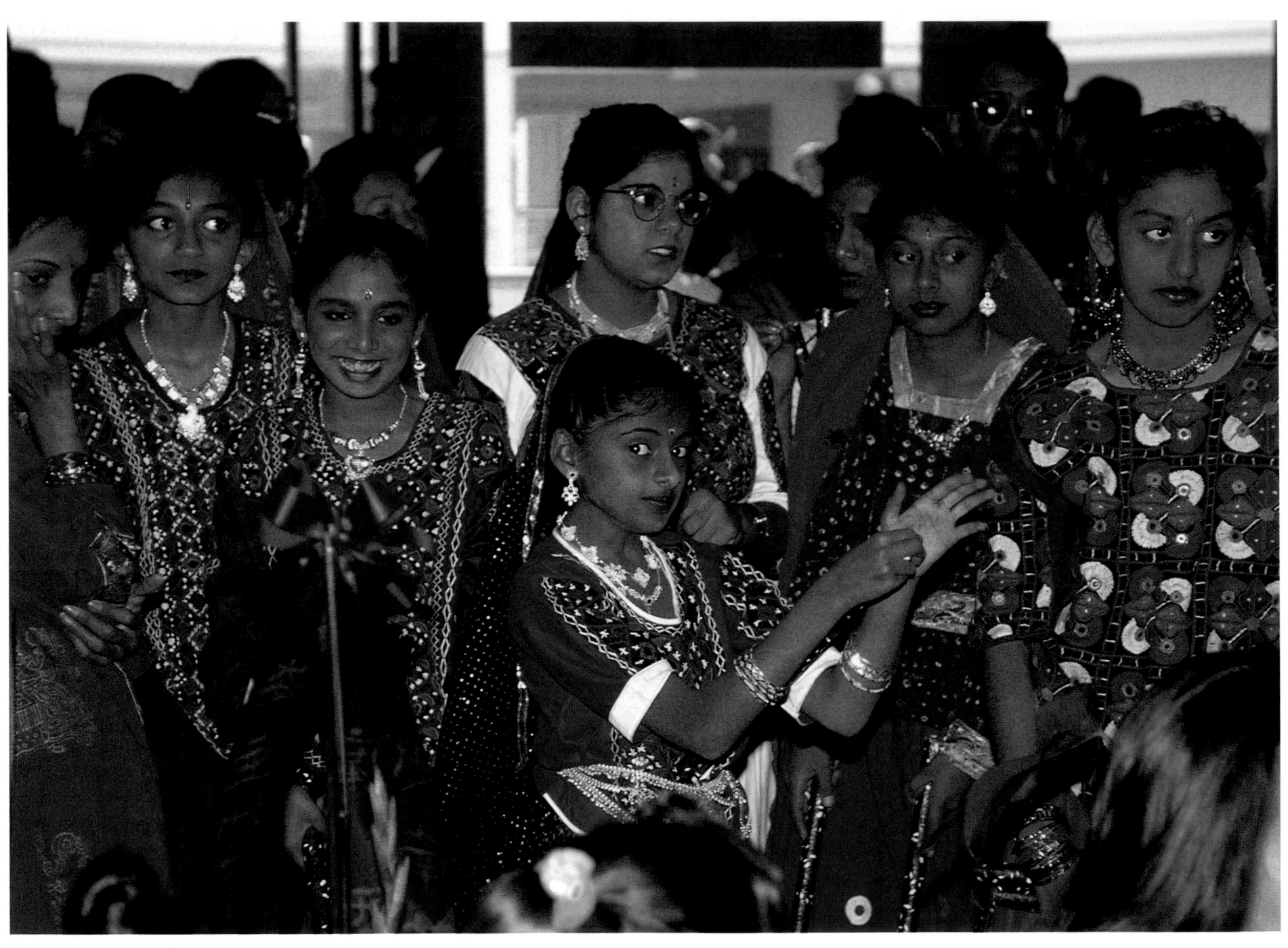

At the dedication of the Asian Cultural Center   Chinatown   *February 1994*

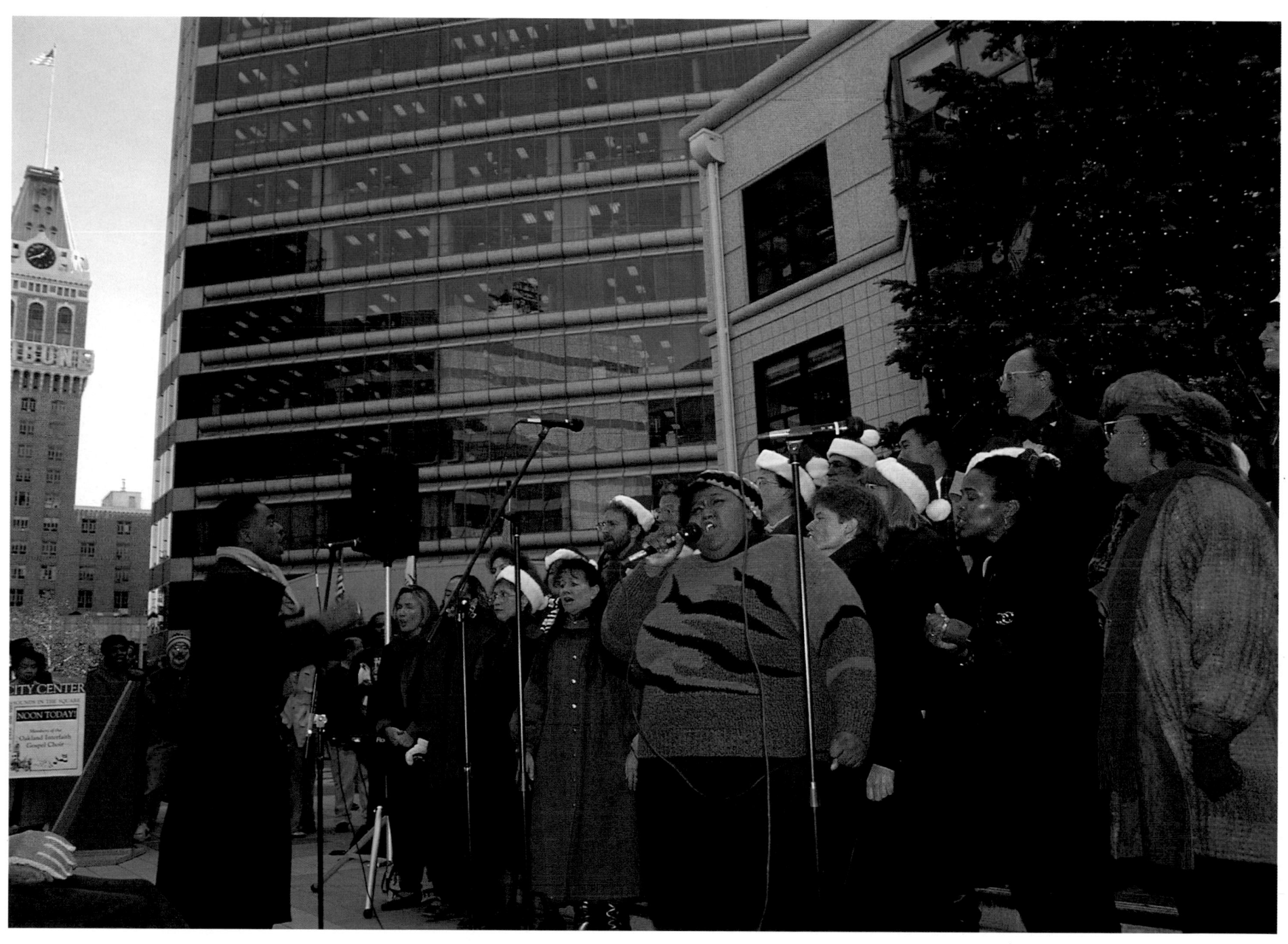

Members of the Oakland Interfaith Gospel Choir   City Center Plaza   *December 1992*

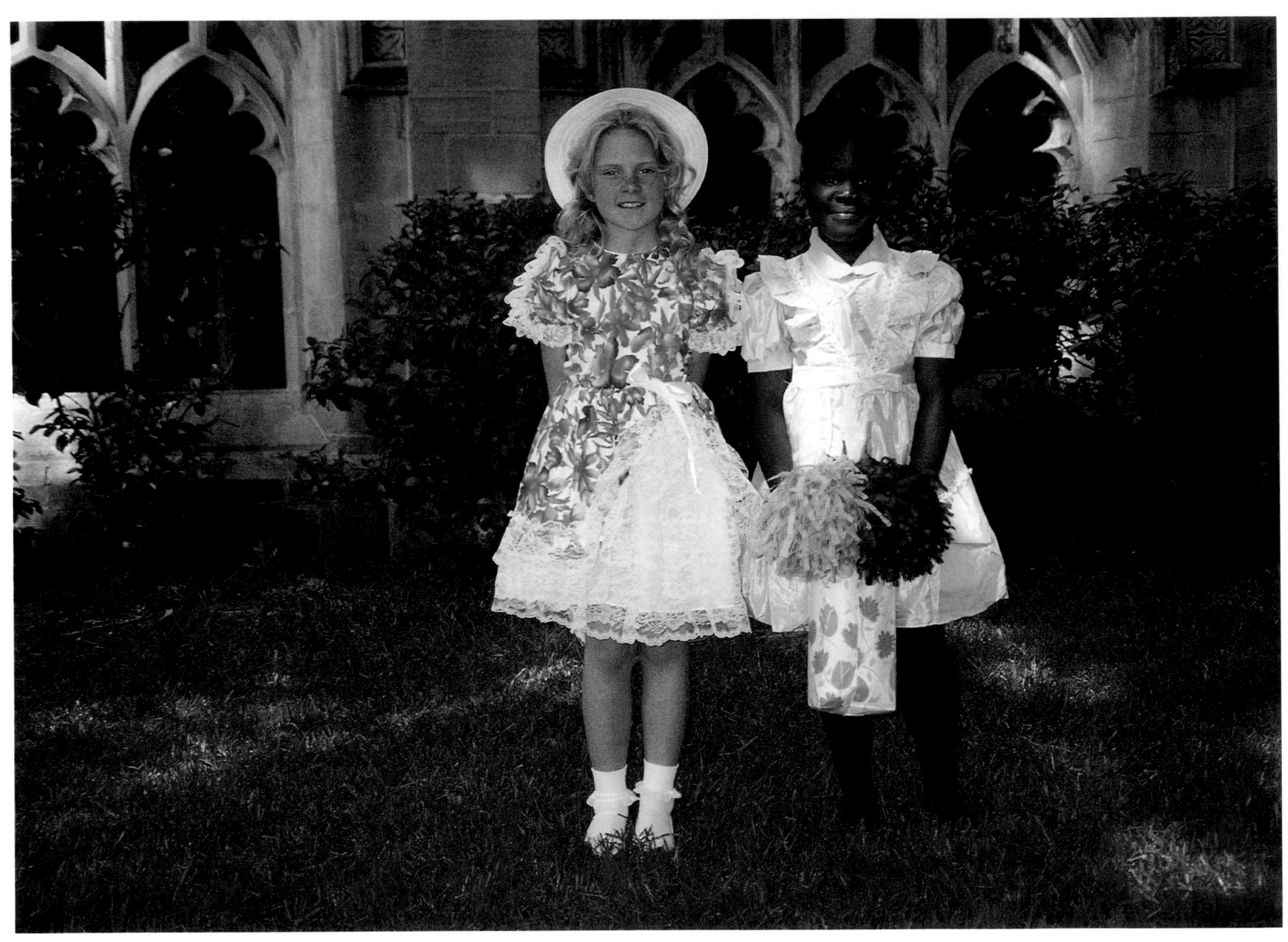

After Easter Sunday Services   First Presbyterian Church of Oakland, 27th and Broadway   *April 1993*

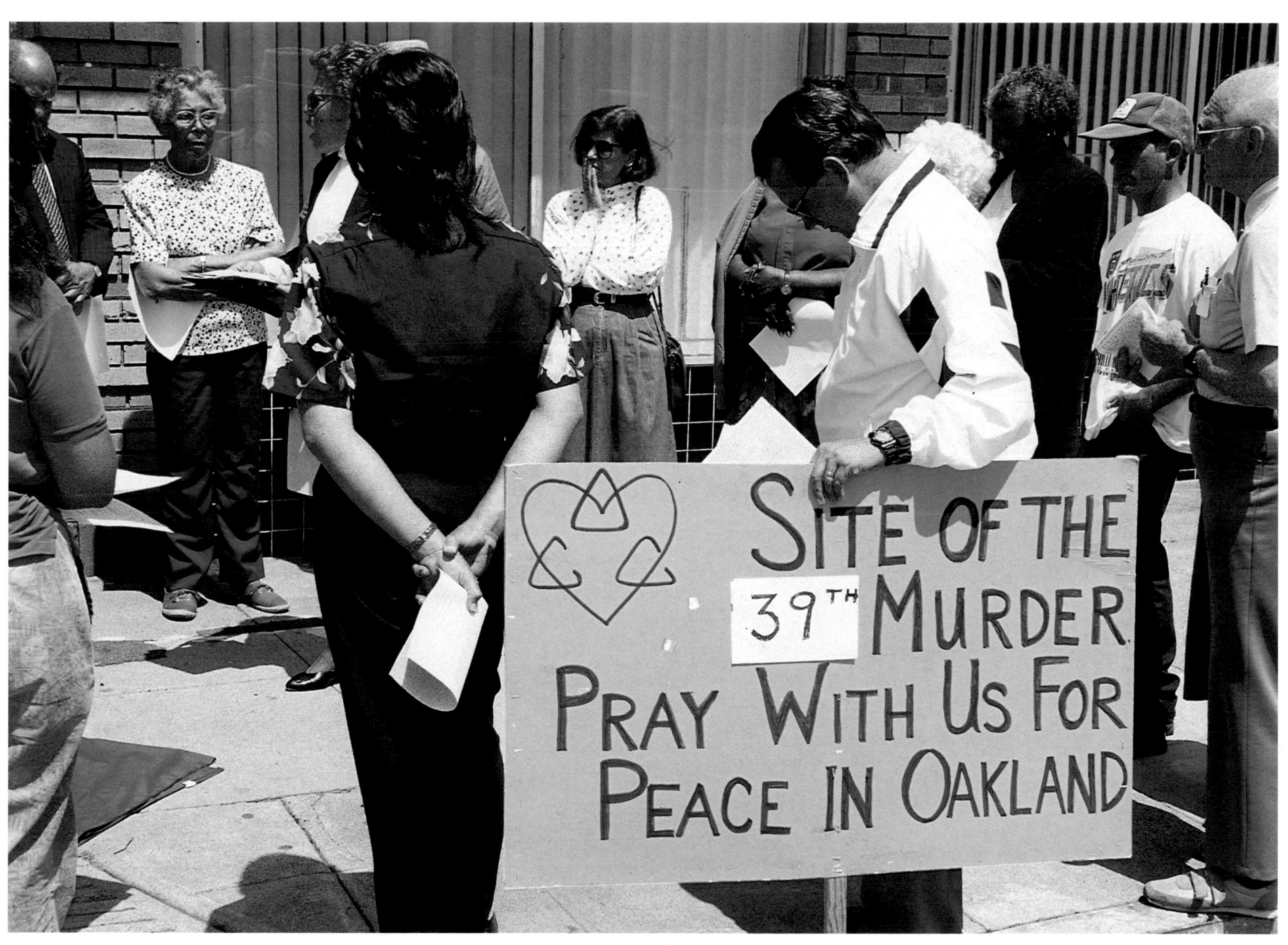

Memorial   Martin Luther King Jr. Way   *May 1993*

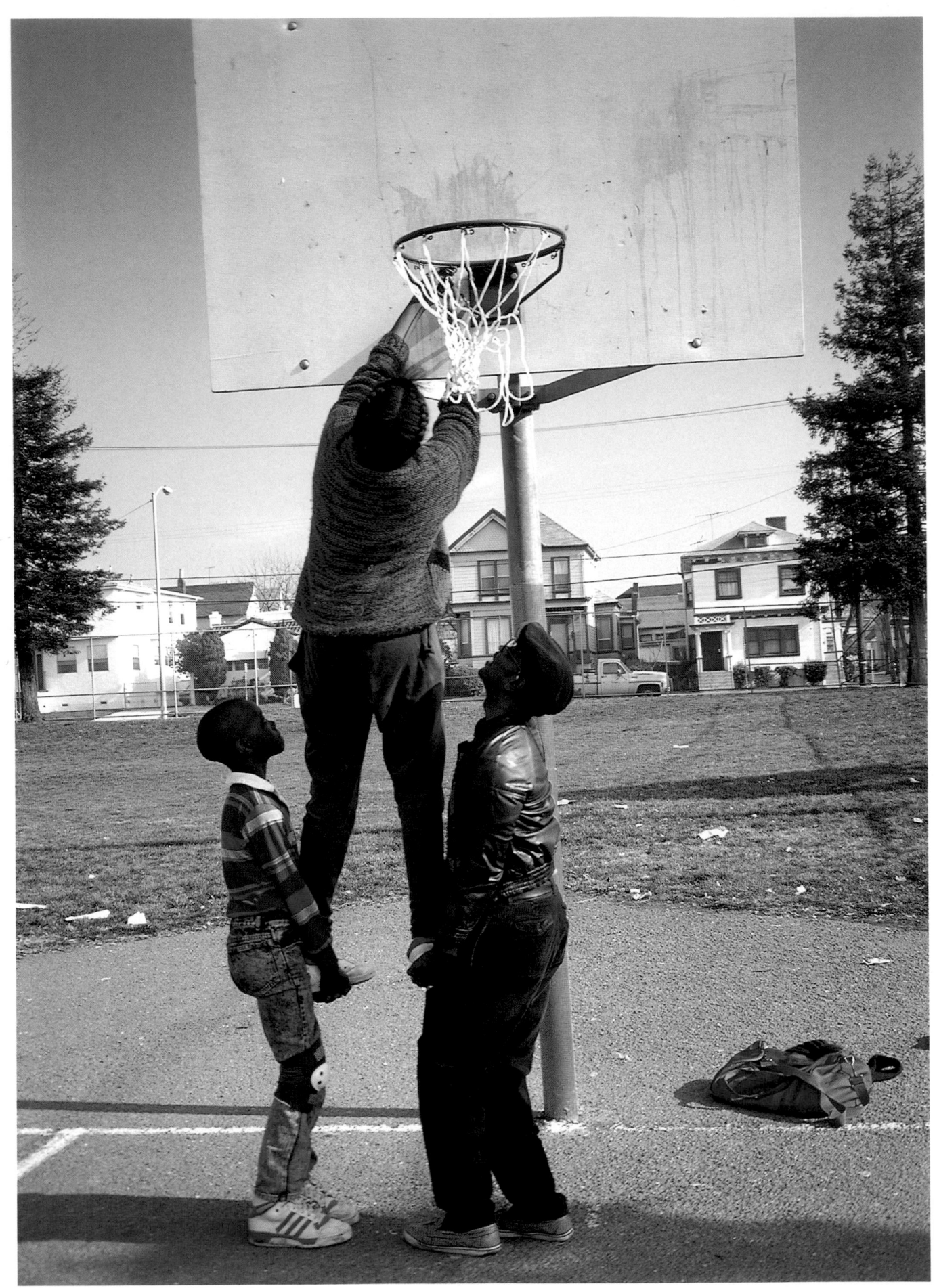

Hanging the net   16th and Adeline   *January 1989*

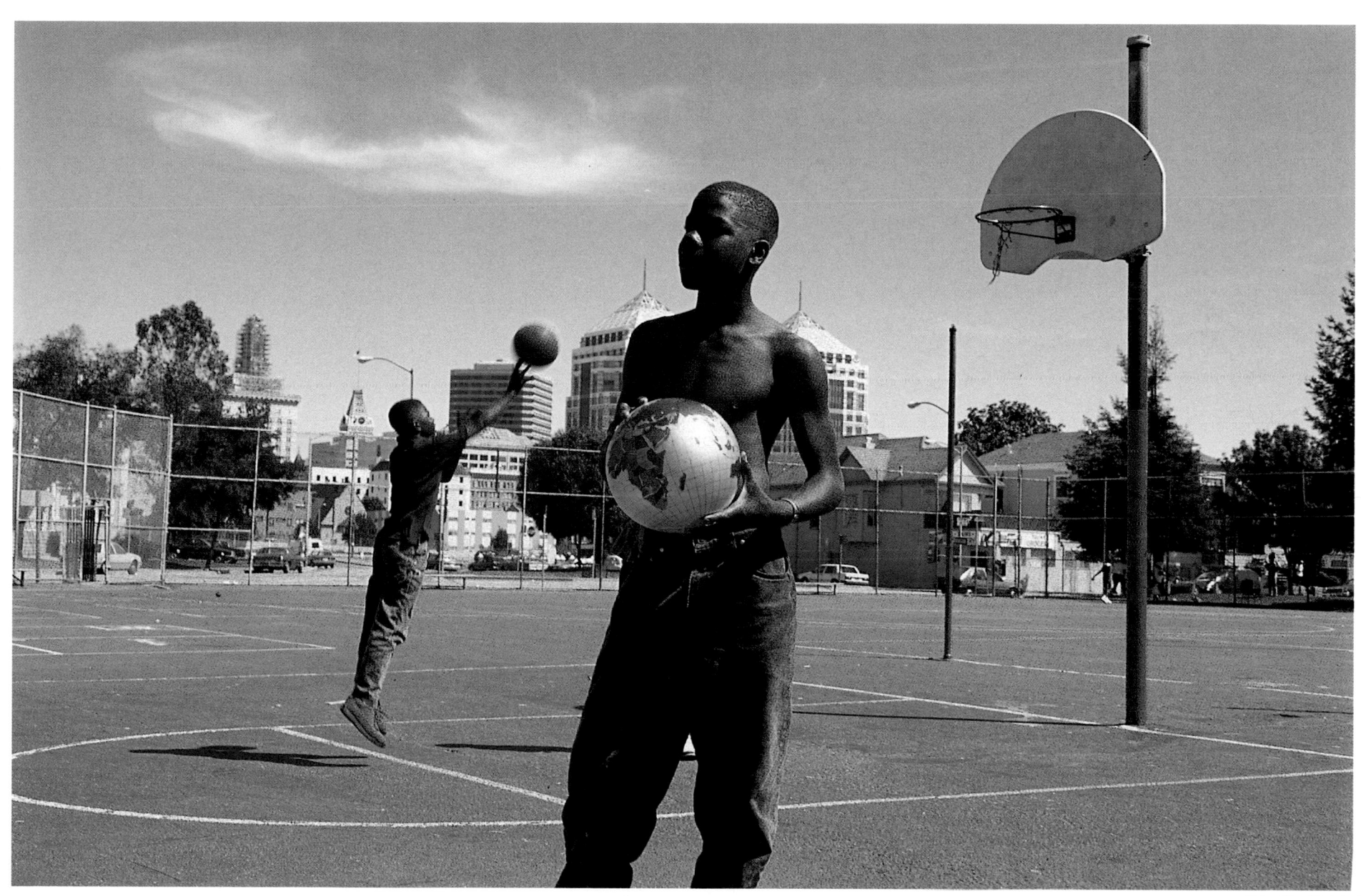

Oakland and the world   18th and West   *May 1993*

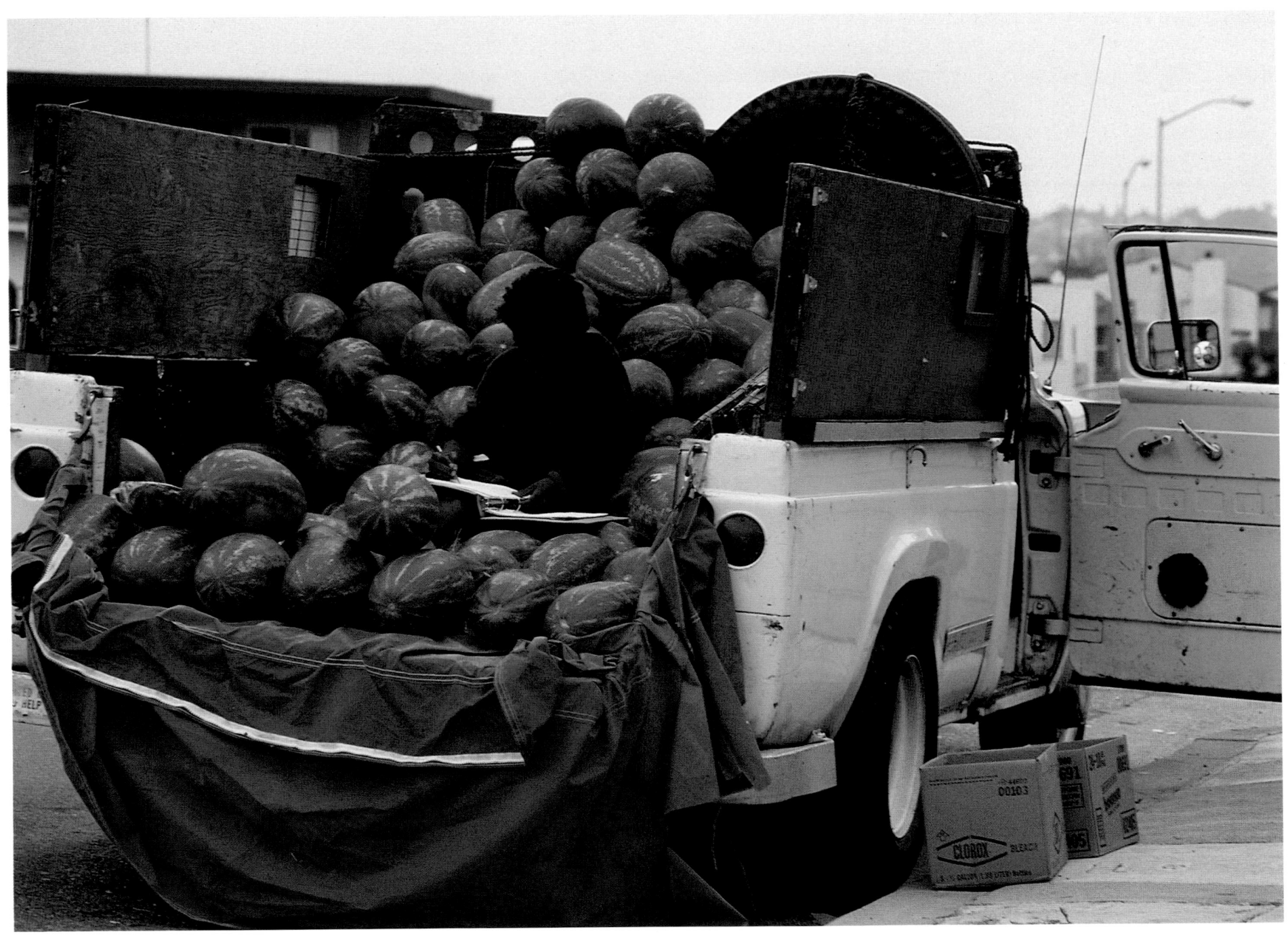

Homework   16th and Market   *August 1983*

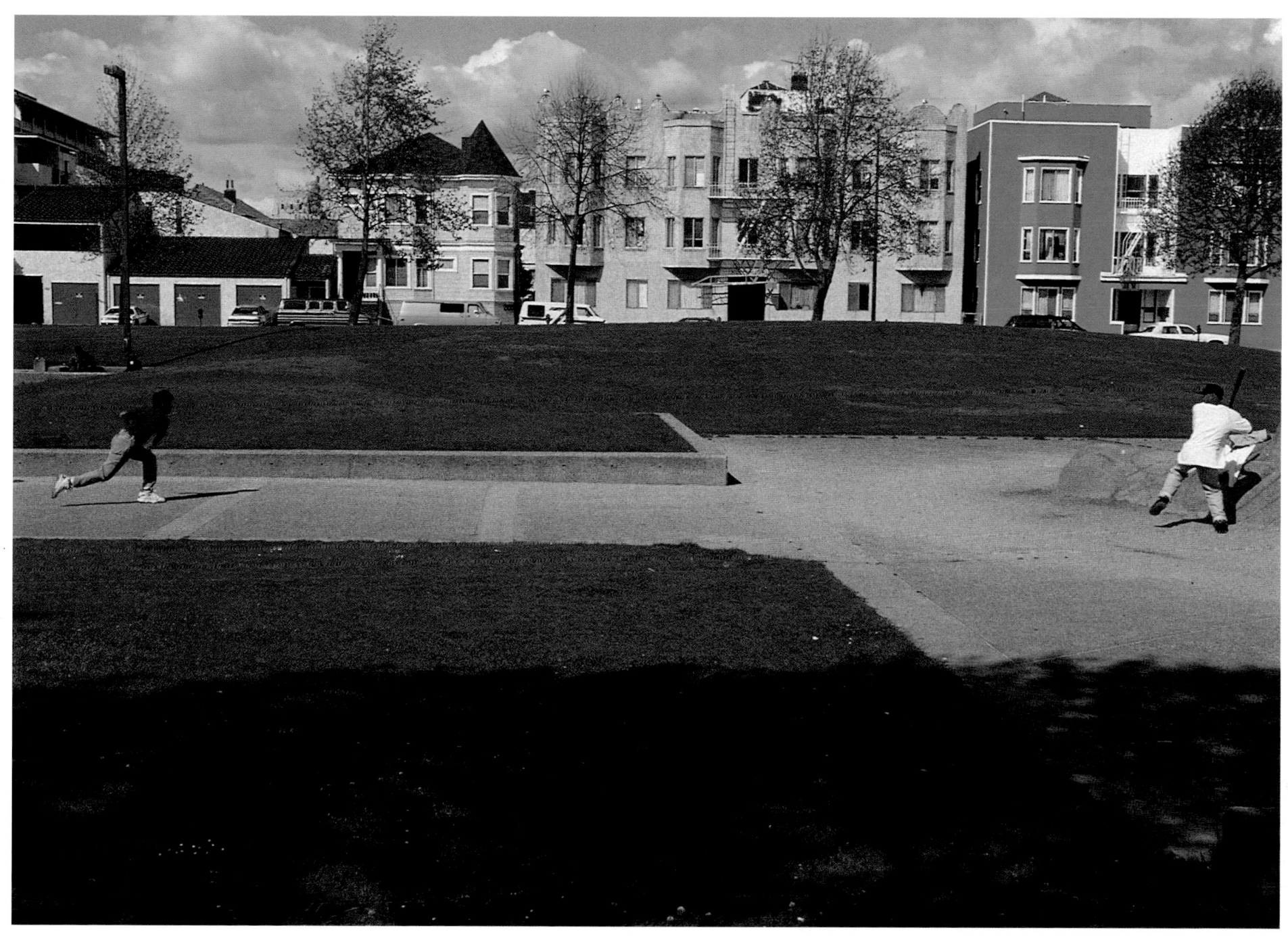

Spring training in Chinatown   8th and Madison   *April 1994*

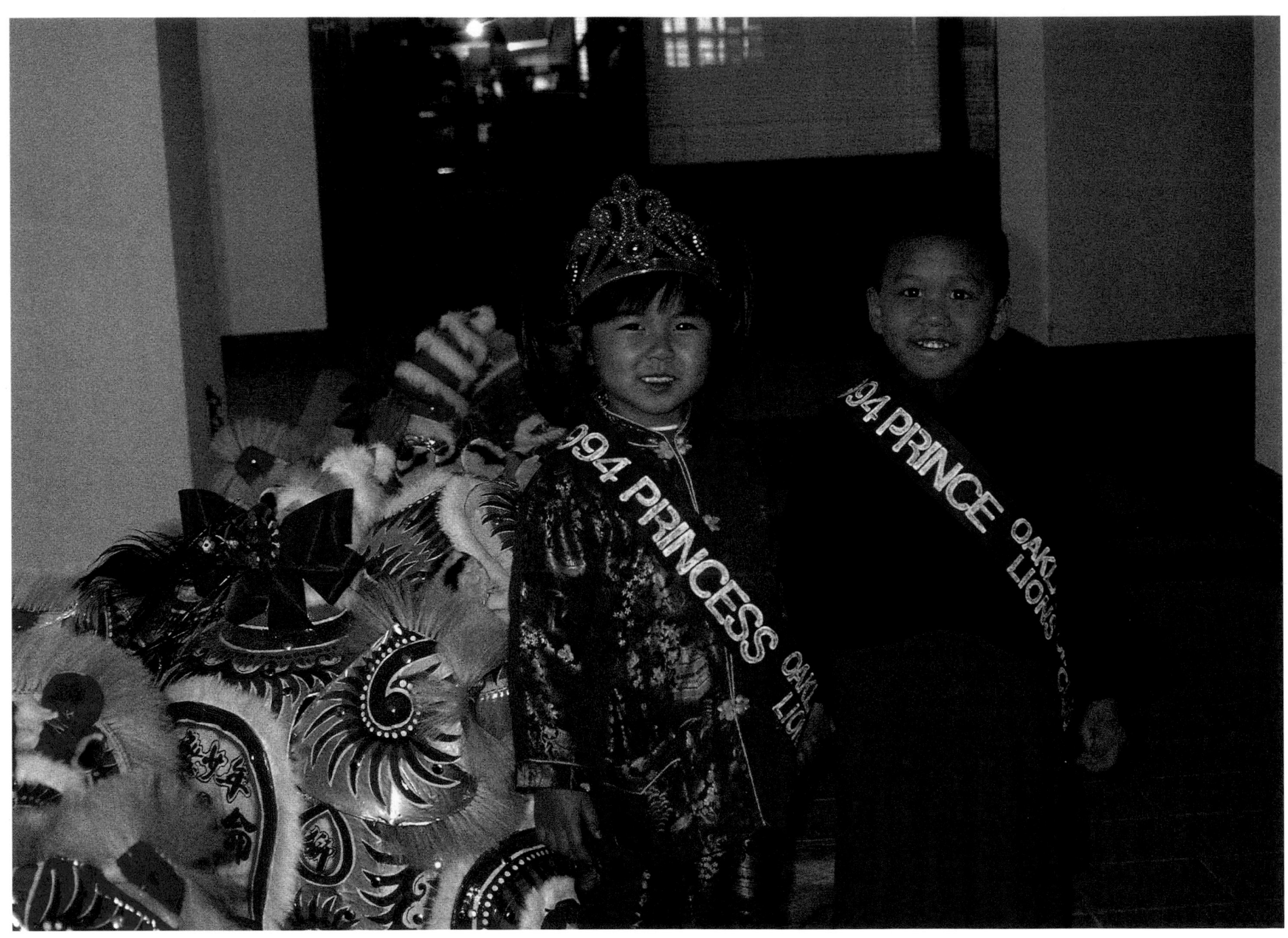

Prince and Princess   Chinatown   *February 1994*

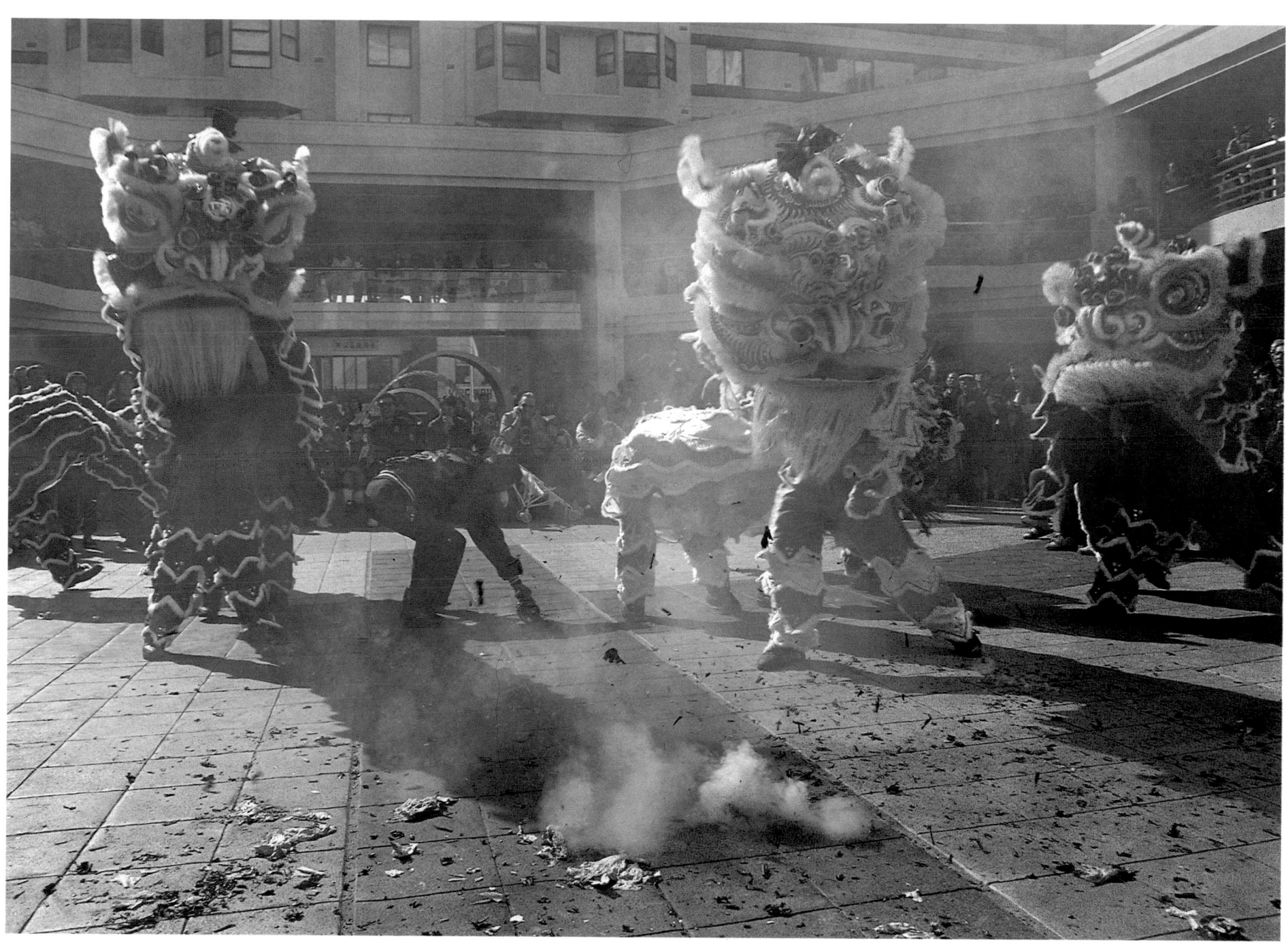

New Year's celebration   Chinatown   *February 1994*

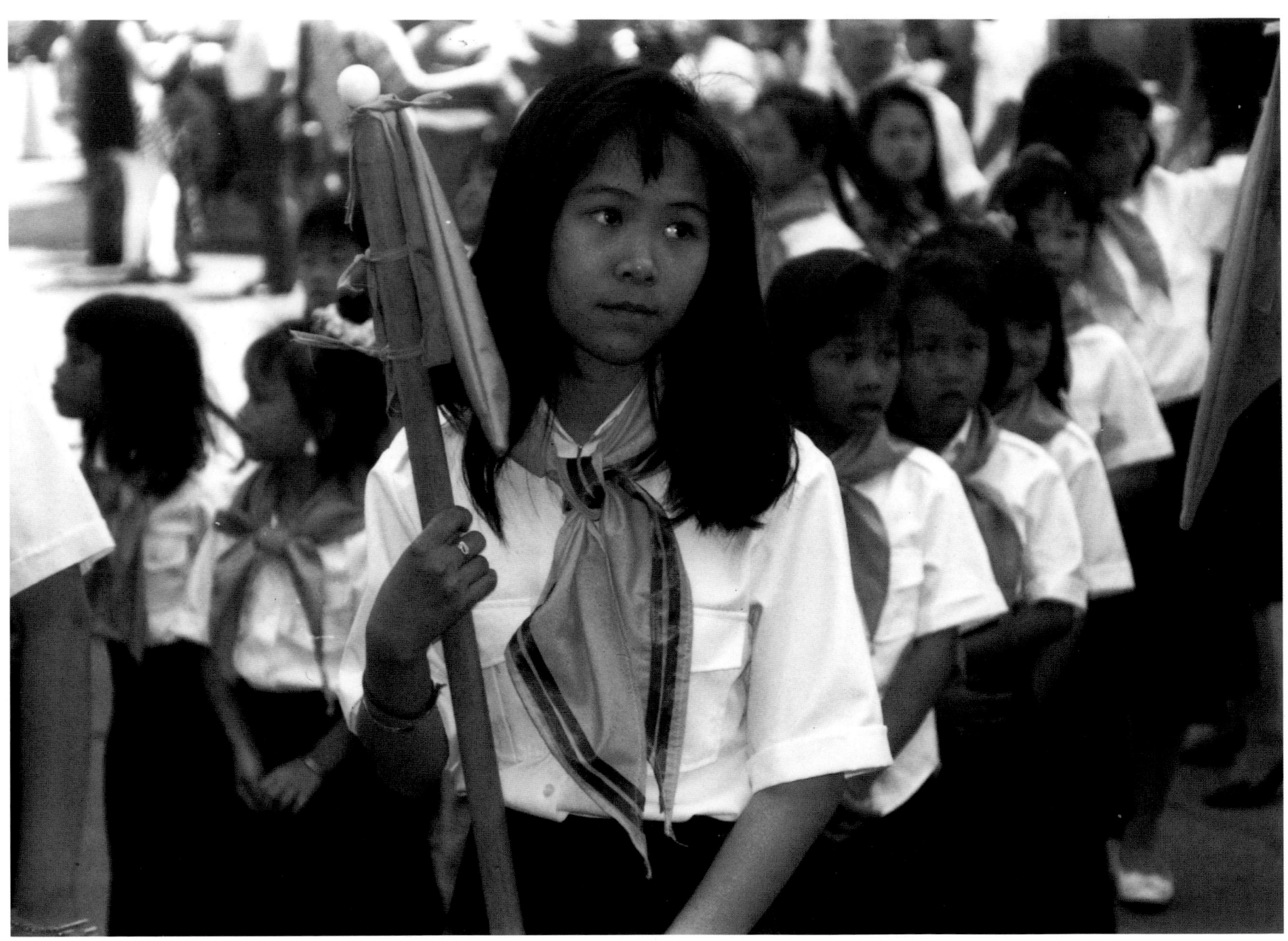

Vietnamese Girl Scouts   7th and Martin Luther King Jr. Way   *June 1991*

Sunset at Lake Merritt   *November 1992*

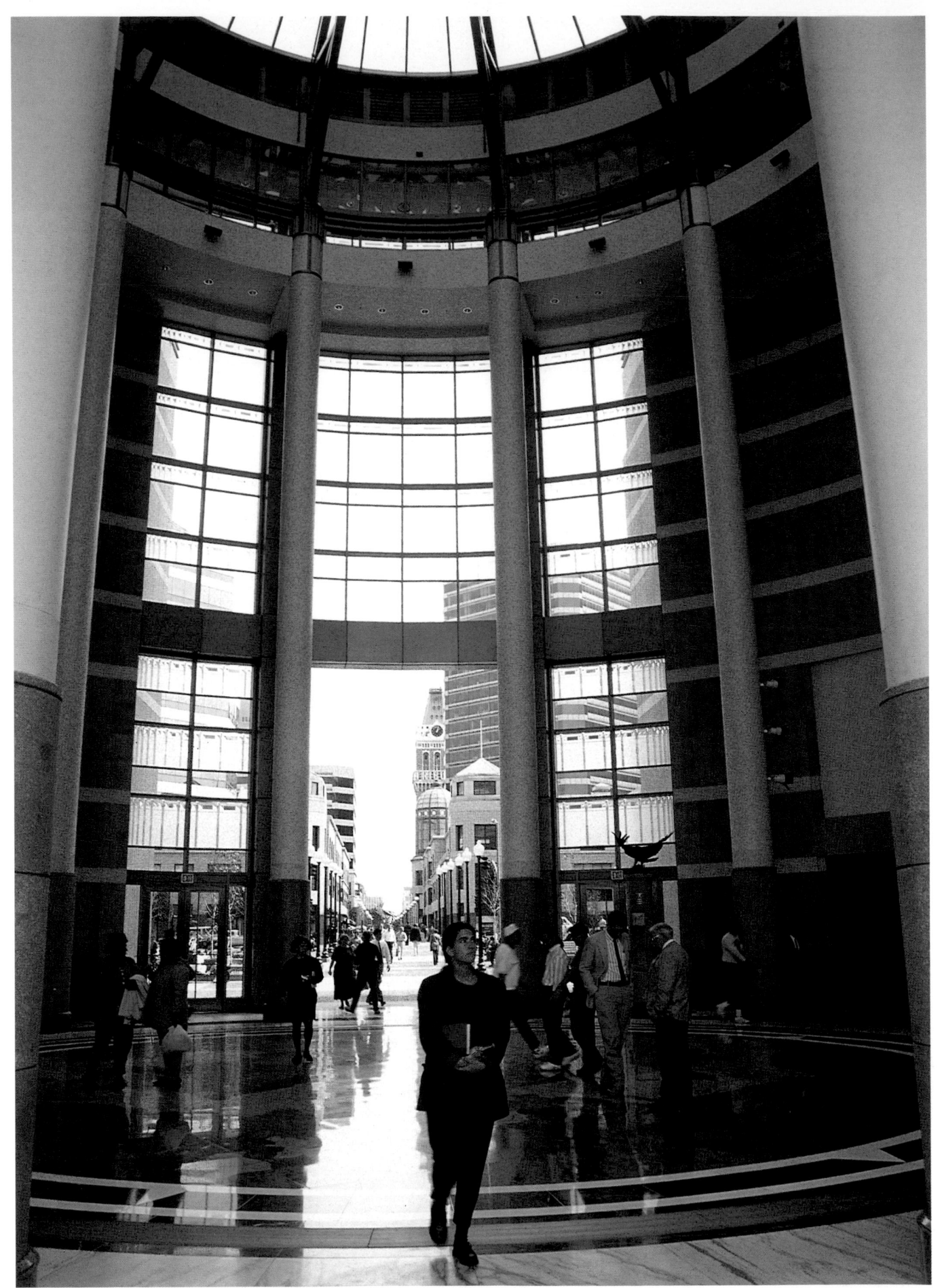

Lobby of the Federal Building *March 1994*

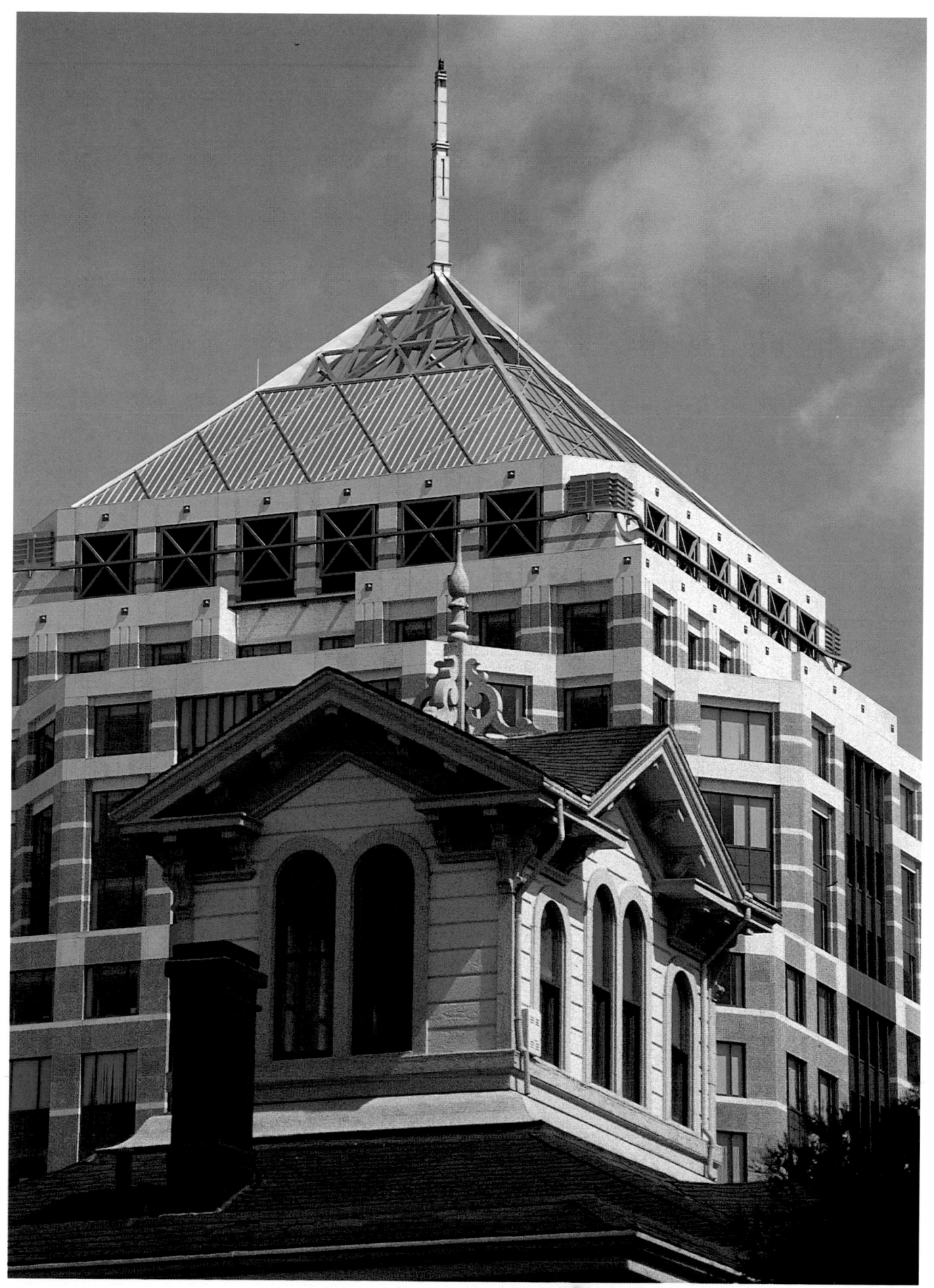

The Pardee Home Museum and the Federal Building   from 11th and Castro   *April 1994*

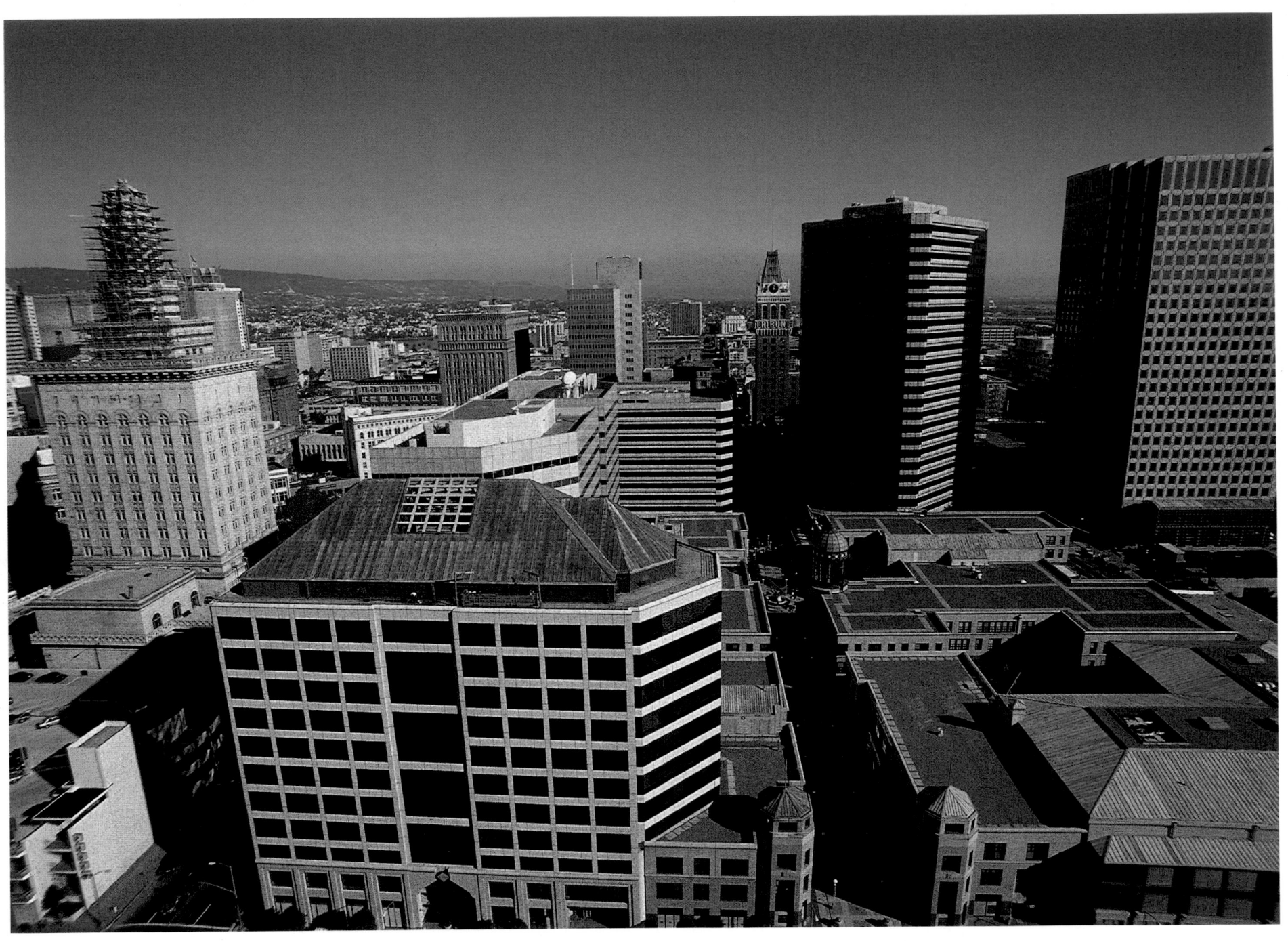

The Oakland hills from the Federal Building *October 1993*

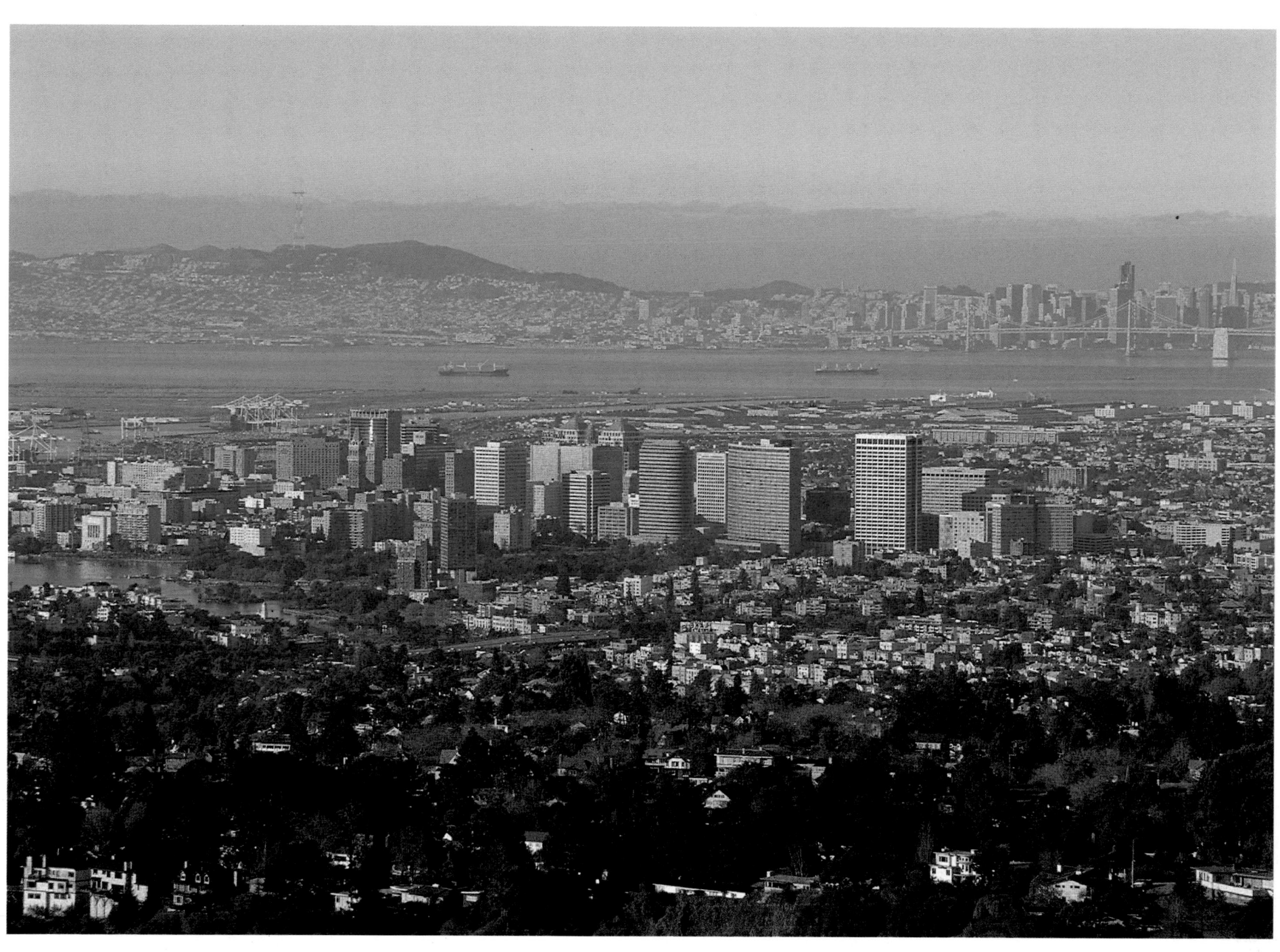

Looking back the other way   *December 1993*